Living before DYING

God's Peace

Jack †

Living
before
DYING

Reflections of a Hospice Chaplain

❧

Rev. Mr. Jack Conrad

Tate Publishing & *Enterprises*

Published by Tate Publishing & Enterprises, LLC
127 E. Trade Center Terrace | Mustang, Oklahoma 73064 USA
1.888.361.9473 | www.tatepublishing.com

Tate Publishing is committed to excellence in the publishing industry. The company reflects the philosophy established by the founders, based on Psalm 68:11,
"The Lord gave the word and great was the company of those who published it."

Book design copyright © 2008 by Tate Publishing, LLC. All rights reserved.
Cover design by Janae J. Glass
Interior design by Amber Lee

Published in the United States of America

ISBN: 978-1-60604-694-4
1. SELF-HELP, Personal Growth, Happiness
08.12.02

DEDICATION

I dedicate this first to my wife Linda, the love of my life, my biggest supporter and believer and critic. I also dedicate this book to all the hospice workers who provide the touch of God in all that they do. Finally, to all who have given their life stories to me, written here or not. I sat at their feet and have learned about living before dying.

TABLE OF CONTENTS

FOREWORD

As a hospice chaplain, Jack Conrad looks into dying faces every day. Through latter stages of living and dying, Jack journeys with hospice care patients and their families and helps them to find relief for a grief unresolved, joy in a remembrance long buried, or a generative course of action which, however simple, may have profound meaning. As much as is humanly possible, he enables others to enter into a quality of life that is at once awesome and terrifying. In The Idea of the Holy, Rudolf Otto characterized this as a tremendous mystery, that is, a mysterium tremendum.

Two years ago in a course on monasticism, I assigned students to do a weekly reflection paper or some other response to themes or questions arising from *Jesus, the Teacher Within* by Benedictine writer Laurence Freeman. Jack chose to offer stories that grew out of his interaction with his hospice care clients and his reading of Freeman, Joan Chittister, Thomas Merton, Judith Sutera, and other monastic writers. In each story Jack enabled class participants to experience each situation as very real and to achieve something our culture generally does not encourage, namely, to explore the impact of death on our lives.

Jack elevated an assignment from the ordinary to another plane. I was not alone in encouraging him to continue to write. Subsequently, a chorus of voices has reinforced Jack's commitment to the spiritual discipline of writing. We see the fruit of his story-telling *in Living Before Dying: The Impact of Death on Our Lives.* With an economy of words, a quality of good storytelling, Jack shares encounters in such a way that readers are able to move beyond his or her own emotions to parallel situations in their own lives. As I have read and re-read these stories, I have been moved to remember family and friends with whom I have interacted, especially toward the end of life, and to be re-membered with that family and friends, some long deceased. To give a theological expression to this experience, Jack has imparted to me a fresh encounter of what Christians call of the communion of saints, that great company of the living and the dead with whom I remain inescapably linked in the living of my days.

Without elaborating at length, Jack uses as back-bone for his stories categories of Gary Gunderson and Larry Pray in *Leading Causes of Life.* These are connection, coherence, agency, blessing, and hope. Encouraging readers to see how death impacts the living, he wants us to draw from each vignette insights about our own relationships, about the sources of meaning in our lives, and about what might be birthed as we continue on from life to a realm beyond life as we know it. Like a pebble thrown into a pond, each story has the possibility of touching something deep within our lives, to acknowledge what is precious, and to transform whatever we may need to act upon.

In contemporary words of the creed of the United Church of Canada, we are not alone. We live in God's world. In life, in death, in life beyond death, God is with us. Thanks to God!

INTRODUCTION—THE PREMISE

Death Matters in Life

As a hospice chaplain I have the opportunity to look into the face of life just prior to death. Unfortunately I also have seen a great many faces of death in the living. The miracle of life is amazing. We wake up each morning. If we are fortunate, we see, hear, smell, taste and touch with an ease that becomes too commonplace. We accept it as something expected.

We can breathe with ease, enjoy the warmth of the sun, or brace at the feel of a brisk breeze in the winter. All this comes usually without effort or thought. Life, the process of living, can lose value usually as we get older, just because we do not see the miracles around us. The wonder of what life was like as a baby, or as a toddler, is replaced somehow. We fall into a trap and accept that life is, what it is, and that it will always will be exactly as it is today, except we get older.

But that is not true. When death enters into our comfortable little world, either our own, or someone who is dear to us, or due to horrific acts like a tsunami, or war, we are caught unaware, shocked, and bewildered. We are thrown off balance. The foundation of our very being is rocked, sometimes for a short time, sometimes forever. Death even in the old still amazes us that it shows up at all. Death matters in life.

I remember an earthquake in southern California some years ago that created substantial damage and loss of life. During the earthquake my daughter described the parking lot as rolling like waves on the sea, as she held on to a pillar on a building. To my daughter, the very solid ground that she walked on, at that moment, was never quite solid again. There was now a knowing that the ground we walk upon is not solid at all. It can move and consume and harm us. Although I did not experience it in seeing the parking lot roll, her telling it to me through her twelve-year-old eyes shook my foundations also. The fear, the awesomeness, and the unreality of it was both exciting and terrifying.

Death is like that earthquake. It is unexpected, and it rocks our foundations, and it can ever leave us changed.

I chose to write this project, to discuss the significant impact that death has on life and the significant impact that life has on death. Having now experienced this with many, many families, as suddenly they face the fact that we all know–we are going to die–I think it is important to tell these stories. Some may touch you, and cause you to pause and think. Some may bring back memories of a loved one who has died or is dying in your life. It may trigger a grief unresolved, or a remembrance long buried. If that occurs, this book has served its purpose.

I caution the reader. There are some stories that are hard to read, and moving. If you need to take it slow, and read only a few stories at a time, that's okay. But I suggest you persevere. It is tolerable.

I hope this project will provide insight to new people in pastoral care or in hospice. This is so that they can better see, and hopefully understand, the "dying community." This, as well as affirmation and identity to those that have served or are serving those confronted with death.

First, we do have some choices to make, or things to look for in life and death. Before we look at stories, let's look at a way of looking at life.

LEADING CAUSES OF LIFE

and the Structure of Telling these Stories

Dr. Gary Gunderson and Larry Pray, in their book *Leading Causes of Life*, I believe address a very interesting question–What are the causes of life?

We, as people in this world, tend to seek to understand usually only the causes of death. Why does cancer do what it does? Why does the heart weaken? How does stroke occur, what effect does it have on the survivor? All good, solid questions. However, if we look rather at the causes of life, maybe life can be embraced, be longer, and be more important than trying to postpone death. Life is caused by healthy practices but is also caused by the way we live our life and important ways in which life comes to us.

Gary and Larry cite five main causes. They full well acknowledge that there may be more, but they have concluded that five causes can be isolated. These are connection, coherence, agency, blessing and hope.

Leading Causes of Life–Core Categories (from summary insert to *Leading Causes of Life*)

Connection: The web of relationships that nurture, sustain, and serve as a resource for healing; the social fabric of persons' lives (e.g. family, friendship, vocational, social, and religious bonds) which can serve as transformative networks for persons, families, and communities.

Coherence: Meaning and belonging, "…a master narrative held so deeply that it goes beneath language and into consciousness…an assumption that life holds together in the face of the most difficult and horrible circumstances."

Agency: The capacity to act, "…a generative force that inevitably leads to the matter of call. It gives traction to three questions: 'What am I to do with my life? What have I been called to do? Am I doing it?'" Doing that goes beyond activity as such.

Blessing: Affirmation of another at a deep, primal level of being; blessing can be given or received from another, but one cannot bless oneself; integral to blessing are connection, coherence, and agency; thus blessing leads to action and hope seeking healing change with others.

Hope: More than wishful thinking, hope is leaning into the future with anticipation fully aware of reality; a process rather than an event where one thrives in the midst of whatever challenges and adversity is at hand; "riskable expectation."

I am not going into any great discussion on these, but I am choosing to use these as a backbone for my stories. Some exhibit the cause, some the lack of the cause. Some exhibit many of the causes. It does provide a way to look at these real-life encounters with death, and perhaps learn from these experiences.

LOSS

One other underlying knowledge is that Loss occurs to those who are in the dying community a little at a time. It is rarely radical unless in a tragic accident. I would like to use the six general categories of loss as expounded by Mitchell and Anderson in their 1983 book *All Our Losses, All Our Grief: Resources for Pastoral Care.* Each of the dying will experience many losses. Each loss will be a small loss, and each loss will rob them of some form of life. We all go through these losses as we age. But many in these stories have experienced all of these losses as they prepare for death. Here are those losses, with a very brief explanation. The key for the person dying is that each loss is something to be grieved about, and must be grieved about.

Material Loss–the loss of assets, both financial as well as keepsakes.

Relational Loss–the ending of the ability to have personal intimacy with those who are valued. This is very important to those who survive those who die.

Intrapsychic Loss–the loss of a dream or ideal. Very relevant to the dying is the loss of the idea that we are "healthy" people. All the things that were yet to be done.

Functional Loss–the loss of the functioning of the body. As each stage of loss of function, it is one more thing lost and to be grieved over.

Role Loss–the loss one feels of having been the one in charge of earning money or taking care of tasks around the house. It can be the role of a parent who now is more in the "child" role.

Systemic Loss–the loss of systems that once were important to you. It can be associations one belonged to, or church, or clubs, that no longer can be visited or attended.

You will see "loss" in each of these stories; not just death, but losses of life that we, the healthy, take for granted. I add these to increase the sensitivity perhaps of the reader as they encounter these people's stories.

One other piece that I use is a study that is ongoing on the power of *regret* in the dying. Based on a recent study by the University of Memphis in conjunction with Methodist Alliance Hospice, *regrets* are a part of the end of life review that are named by most of the dying in the study. *Regrets* are those things in our lives that we do, and regret, or do not do, and regret. You will see expressions of regret as you journey through the stories.

THE STORIES

All of my stories are based on real encounters. Mostly they are mine. The names and facts may not be perfectly accurate and/or factual; some of this is by design to keep confidentiality. But some of it is because, over time, it has allowed me perhaps a different insight or remembrance. But the stories carry the message, and I have attempted to be true to the people who lived them and died them, without too much alteration.

I also tell my story, as I was part of their story. This is the way in which I am coming to see life and death. Although I will quote others, these are mainly my experiences, or personal perceptions. Sometimes, with the permission of others, I have used their stories. I have also put in a few stories that speak to the cause of life that I may be highlighting. These stories have touched me and carry a message. I have written them as they were told to me. I thank each of the chaplains and friends that have given me a story.

Well, here we go.

ALL THE LEADING CAUSES—

Two Composite Stories

Life has a language. If we are to find our lives on this violent, troubled planet, we must learn the language of life.

Gary Gunderson with Larry Pray,
Leading Causes of Life

There is always one cause of life that is prominent in most stories. It seems to stand out or be spoken by the person or family and their underlying story. However, two stories I feel exemplify the best blending of, or lack of, all the causes of life. I choose these to kind of get the concepts of the causes of life across to the reader.

I introduce you now to the real living and dying in life, to help "learn the language of life."

What are you waiting for?

A man should not leave this earth with unfinished business.

Diane Frolov and Andrew
Schneider, *Northern Exposure,*
"All is Vanity," 1991.

The care and concern that Tish gave to Stu was real and heartfelt. Her eyes were so fixed upon his, her hand held his with such tenderness, there was time spent there between them that sought expression, of acceptance and love. She listened with intent as Stu spoke of the times that they had shared. The party where she got embarrassed, where the straps on her dress came undone. The time at the beach. It came from him easily to me, telling of his life with Tish. They shared laughter.

I was glad that I finally was able to meet and spend time with this woman, his girlfriend. I had heard about Tish so often from Stu. His love for her was rich and deep. As a hospice chaplain, I often just hear of loved ones, during our day visits, and too often miss those that determine the "living of life" to terminal patients. To Stu, Tish was his heart. And he knew that his life was drawing to a close. The pain was more severe now; the medication was robbing him of lucid hours, being traded for sleep.

The brain tumor increased its size, demanding more space, insisting; inoperable the doctors said.

On the next visit, we spoke of Tish, and what she meant to him. He related with laughter and tears the last twenty years of their relationship. As so often happens in me, I feel something welling inside of me, and I know it is a question that demands to be asked. It is rarely an easy question; some might say it is a personal, almost too private question of the patient. It is a question that is meant only to be discussed between profound friends. When such questions rise, I have learned to "go with them," not wanting to regret the opportunity missed. So, when the conversation lagged, I said, "Stu, I saw a love between you and Tish that was really remarkable. You two share something that is powerfully real."

Stu looked hard at me; a small smile crept over the left side of his face, the part not being affected by the tumor. "I guess we do. We have loved each other in a way I never thought possible. I thought I loved my first wife. But I think I wasn't ready to love enough. I was too caught up in being a policeman. It didn't work, more my fault than hers. But Tish has had my heart since we met. Oh, we can fight, but we certainly know how to love." Stu chuckled. "I am a lucky man, Jack."

"How long have you two been together?" I asked.

"It's been twenty years last April," Stu reflected as he stared off a bit, as if remembering her fragrance and expressions on the day that they met.

"Can I ask you a question, Stu?" Stu nodded. "How come you guys never got married?" I asked.

This stopped him. Stu and I had shared many times on his faith, and the power that God had in his life. He was a faithful man, devoted to family and to God, and so it seemed this piece of his life was just a bit out of place. I presumed his divorce was difficult, but we had not spoken in detail about it.

"I guess because I never asked her," Stu spoke softly. " I know why. We both were afraid to be hurt again. And I wanted to make sure I never hurt her, like I did my first wife." He paused. "And I didn't want to get hurt again, I guess is the real truth. Tish is so good to me. I guess I always thought she deserved better than me. I had always planned on doing it some day."

After a moment of quiet, I said, "What are you waiting for?"

"I don't know. This is crazy. " Stu spoke, and then the half smile returned to his face.

"Do you think she would say yes?" I asked.

"I would hate to put that on her, but ..." He trailed off and wandered into thought.

"Stu, you don't have to do anything, and you seem to be in a good place with the Lord. God certainly isn't going to condemn you if you don't, but I was just wondering."

Stu relaxed against his pillow, and his eyes got heavy.

"Getting tired, my friend?" I asked.

Stu nodded.

"Would you like to share a prayer before I go?"

"How about you just pray for me, Chaplain? I am really tired. Those pills are hitting me. I am going to sleep a bit." With that he fell asleep. I quietly asked God to help this man as his days started to dwindle. As I was leaving the room, I heard my name called. I looked back toward Stu, who was lying there with his eyes closed. He quietly said, "Thank you."

Two days later, when I was in the midst of a meeting, my cell phone went off. I knew that Stu could go at any time, so I excused myself from my meeting and answered my phone. It was Stu. "When can you do the wedding, Chaplain? I don't have much time, you know." Deep warmth penetrated my heart. I laughed heartily. She had said yes and had cried with joy.

The next day I spoke with Tish on the phone and checked it all out. She was in a good place with this, and I told her this would put a whole new dimension to her grief. She realized that, but was willing to wed the man she had loved for twenty years. She said it was if she were living in a dream.

Tish and Stu were married the next Monday afternoon. The ceremony was held in the bedroom. He trimmed his mustache and hair. Family was there, a big cake, and the vows exchanged, "till death do us part."

Stu went into a final stretch with his tumor later that week, became almost comatose, and died two weeks later, peacefully with Tish and his family around him. In our last exchange, they both told me that they were glad they married in spite of the circumstances. His last words to me were, "Thank you, Chaplain. You are God's vessel."

The funeral was one of the most difficult, but yet one of the most meaningful that I had ever done or attended. Tish was overwrought with her grief, a newlywed, a wife, and now a widow. Done with full knowledge, done out of love, sacrificial love.

Death is more about living than dying. Death is a moment in all of our lives, if we are lucky, that allows us to define ourselves, our purpose, and our relationships. We can easily choose to die without living, and I have seen too many lives like that. We are told that one of the key elements of the dying process, if we are given some time, is to reflect on regrets. The regrets for things we have done, and the regrets of things that we have not done. Stu and Tish taught me two things. First, don't die with regrets. Live out life, do what needs to be done, without allowing past hurts to be barriers to a life fully lived. Take the chance, find out if what you desire possesses magic for you.

And second, they taught me to always ask the difficult question, not only of patients, but of myself.

In this story of Stu and Tish, you can see that the choice Stu made to ask Tish to marry him, covered all the "causes of life." The connection with Tish brought him sustenance. The coherence really has meaning that ties with the description "an assumption that life holds together in the face of the most difficult and horrible circumstances" (Gunderson, insert). What could possibly be more horrible than being bedridden and dying? Yet Stu chose to act because life was still "holding together" for him. With the challenge to act, Stu stepped into Agency, "the capacity to act." He answers the questions posed in Gunderson's definition of Agency, "What am I to do with my life? What have I been called to do? Am I doing it?" When confronted with the question was he doing it, he was called to the capacity to act. Stu and Tish received blessing from each other in "seeking healing change with others." The healing was with both Stu and Tish, in broken relationships of their past, and probably hurts that they had with each other over their twenty years with each other. And of course, Hope. This had to be hard to grab onto that "riskable expectation" that turned out to be only a few weeks, to lean out into the future that was guaranteed to be too short.

You see, these people in their story exemplified the "causes of life." Though for a very short time indeed, they chose life over death. Perhaps it would be good now to look at a less uplifting story, and see that death does impact life, and can have powerful implications for our lives.

Make Her Proud of You.

I am not dying, not any more than any of us are at any moment. We run, hopefully as fast as we can, and then everyone must stop. We can only choose how we handle the race.

Hugh Elliott, Standing Room Only,
06–11–04

Reggie seemed small. Although he was probably big for his age, he seemed small as he sat in the white "Wal-mart-esque" patio chair. His one foot dangled back and forth, back and forth. Maybe it was the situation which made him seem small. Now he was the man of the family, the eldest of the family at eleven.

The room was almost stifling, although it was still cool outside on this late fall evening. Perhaps the house was heated in an attempt to ward off the death of the woman that now lay lifeless in the bed. The heat of the house was no match for the cancer that wracked the poor body of this frail little wisp of a woman, who had lived her full life to the age of twenty-nine. Too young, for such a pretty soul, too young for a woman with a full lifetime ahead of her, too young to have five young children; eleven, nine, six, three, and eighteen months. All with fathers, none who could be verified. This mother was dead.

As I gazed around the room, I saw the blank stares, the disbelief, the worry, the anger, the sadness, in all the faces that occupied that room. There were sisters, a mother, an aunt, a visiting pastoral caregiver from the church, and kids, more than the five that crowded and peered, probably never having seen a dead body before. Some playing and carrying on as if life had not stopped, or death was not a visitor.

Not much was said.

I generally asked for stories of the young woman. I was told that she cared deeply for her children, and even this morning "as sick as she was, she kept them in line." She loved her kids, and loved to sing. "Could she sing. High voice, pretty," her mother spoke as if forcing each word from her mouth.

The door slammed as a man entered the house, quickly glanced into the room where the vigil was being conducted, and stumbled on into the living room of this apartment. When I had entered I noticed two or three men, lying on the floor of that living room. One drinking beer. One passed out. The television droned on about something. The man who entered was unaware of the visitation of death. Life went on.

"She was a good one," the mother of the deceased stated in her monotone voice, "a good one." She stared for a moment at the lifeless body of her youngest child. "A good one." Her eyes closed. Time continued.

I went to the various kids; the oldest daughter, Kisha, nine years old by her own admission, was trying not to cry, as she sat and stared at her momma. I sat next to her and said, "I am sorry, Kisha. I know you will miss her." She continued her stare, and each a traitor to her show of strength, tears streamed down her round cheeks. I offered a hug, and she eagerly took it. But she did not sob.

The nurse arrived to take down all the last-minute data of this life that passed. Chronicling a life gone. Data was necessary for records that would be filed away with the memories. The undertaker called; the slow dance of after-death had begun.

Reggie just sat and stared, that ever-present foot cutting the air with regularity. His eyes went to his mother, then eyes down, then eyes staring forward.

The word went around about Auntie Grace would be taking the kids, it had been decided yesterday, when hope disappeared, God's radical healing would not visit this house, Jesus' tassel had not been touched by this woman. It had been decided. The door opened again, another man, but this one was Will, Uncle Will, who had instantly added five children to his world. Will seemed like a kindly man; perhaps there was hope. But with all I saw, despair was a ocean, and hope was a small canoe.

I asked if I could share a prayer with everyone, the visiting pastoral caregiver from the church readily agreed. I asked her if she wished to pray first. She praised God, and praised His name, she thanked

Him, and prayed with deep sincerity for all in front of her. I too added my prayer, my cry to God for all that remained, as well as for the lovely soul of the young woman. Prayer, sad, real prayer.

As we waited for the hearse to come for what we call so undignified, "the remains," I sat down next to Reggie. Sitting next to the Wal-mart white plastic egg that held Reggie, I had to almost look up at him. He avoided my look, as if knowing that my eyes held a truth that he did not want to see. "Reggie, how ya doing?" No response.

I stared ahead and said, "I have lost my mom too, Reggie, and I miss her still this day, though she has been gone for many years. It still hurts. I am so sorry."

Reggie stared forward; his foot and leg stopped its endless movement, and the only action that came from him then was the tears that rolled down his brown, gentle cheeks, a poor substitute for the kisses once placed on his cheeks by his mother. Then as if from a deeper place that we rarely get to visit, the sobs started, but very quiet, very controlled. Uncle Will, now Daddy Will, looked over his shoulder. His facial expression never changed. But no movement toward Reggie, just a look, and then his face looked at Grace, then he turned and left the room.

Reggie's sobs shook his young body, but no sound now. I reached around and over the mean plastic arm, and placed my arm around the boy, now man. I quietly said over and over, "I am so sorry, I am so sorry." Words are a limited part of who we are, mostly inadequate. His sobs stopped, and for the first time, he looked at me. The sorrow, the fear, the uncertainty, the loss, what does it mean, what will it mean?

I struggled. I have learned that I do not always have the right thing to say. Sometimes, God steps in and jerks a few words from my mouth that are God's, not mine. It was not happening now, but somehow I knew that this moment demanded something, some voice, what it was to be said, I did not know. What do you say to a boy of eleven whose anchor in life, whose stability, main connection, prime supporter, hell, his mother, has died? That one who kept him in line.

My mouth opened as Reggie looked at me, and the phrase came out, "Make your momma proud, Reggie. Make her proud of you." He looked at me with wide eyes, tear-streaked face, and simply nodded. I so rarely use euphemisms, I hate them, but somehow it seemed right. I will never know if I planted a seed, or missed the mark completely.

An eighteen-month-old, Tenisha, jumped in my lap, giggling, blissfully unaware of her mommy being gone. Me, a wonderful plaything on the floor. I hugged her to me in spite of the snot-smeared face, she giggled, I smiled, and we played.

The magic time between Reggie and I had passed, the moment was gone. Sometime in the next few minutes, when I was occupied, he disappeared into the rest of the house, perhaps stepping over the drunk in the living room, to somewhere.

The funeral home came, the body departed. I offered my sympathy and went off to my car. As I glanced back to the door and waved, Reggie's face was there, no wave. As I drove home, I wondered if what I said would change his life for good or ill. I never want to put expectations onto anyone. I do pray he will make his mother proud.

Death demands something from us. It cannot be denied or ignored. It must have a response. We have termed it grief, but it is much more than that. We have to grieve for those we lose, but we also have to "look inside," as Famous Amos said. That looking inside, as we confront death, is looking into our life, and eventual death. Paul Dekar in his book says, "to go down into ourselves is a matter of life and death" (Dekar 177). A response will come in some way. We may submerge it, or treat it with a light touch, but it will seek us out if it is life changing when we lose someone dear. We make choices about the fairness of life, and the gross unfairness of a God that gives life and takes it away.

At eleven, what do we do?

Reggie was living in less than an ideal life already. Probably does not know his father, and the one person in his life, his mother, was now dead. His grandmother seemed to be well along the path to dementia, and Auntie Grace seemed cold, and if she was lucky, she would now be just overwhelmed. Uncle/Daddy was too unknown. Sounds hopeless, and hopelessness is what I felt on my long drive home.

Reggie had connection, lots of family. But would the connection that he had bring him something that, as it said in the definition, "that nurtures, sustains, and serves as a resource for history…which can serve as transformative networks." I think not. Where would he find that connection in his life? Would his connection be like too many other young black men?

Reggie seemed not to have any coherence. How could he? This makes no sense to us as our parents die after a long life, how at eleven, when your mom is twenty-nine. He will have to search for his meaning and belonging.

As for agency, hope and blessing. Those are going to be very hard to find and view in life.

I paint a dismal picture, but this type of story depicts the lack of the causes of life, and can become causes of death. Is Reggie condemned at eleven? I pray not.

I cite this story to depict how death can affect our lives, and can almost demand that we draw on the causes of life to help us cope, help us define ourselves in this lifetime. And so it is with Reggie. As Hugh Elliot said, "We can only choose how we handle the race."

I pray that Reggie chose his race to "make his momma proud."

Let's now take a deeper look at Connection as a cause of life.

CONNECTION

CONNECTION: the web of relationships that nurture, sustain, and serve as a resource for healing; the social fabric of persons' lives (e.g. family, friendship, vocational, social, and religious bonds) which can serve as transformative networks for persons, families, and communities (Gunderson, Insert).

Of all the leading causes of life, I can see connection or the lack of connection so quickly when I encounter people. I guess it is a part of trying to be with people in this crazy world. I have heard the quote, not exactly sure who it was, but it says—We know God the best through our most powerful and meaningful relationships. Gunderson and Pray use the words "fabric" and "networks." I would like to add "web" to the way in which we can look at connection.

Connection in our life deeply bears out as we near death. Far too many people have either outlived or damaged the web of relationships, such that at the time of death, they are quite alone. This is certainly a gift of hospice, to attempt to have no child of God alone at the time of death.

This next story speaks of a deep and lifelong giving connection of two people, where the question arises, "When does our connection end?"

Connection

Will I see Him again?

A family's love lives beyond death.

Camille De Angelis, "Mary Modern"

On of the truths that we as hospice chaplains know is that one of God's favorite forms of entertainment and laughter must be the plans that we make each day. I got the call en route to see another patient. Could I please go and see Herb? As he was actively dying, they wanted a chaplain right away.

When I arrived, the nurse greeted me at the door and said, "It won't be long. His respiration has dropped significantly." Herb was going to die, and soon.

The condo in which Herb and Annie lived was a very nice one. If it weren't for the image of the dying man, in a hospital bed in the middle of the living room, the view of the lake would have been engaging. But what was most striking was Annie bending over Herb, with her full attention on her man. Her eyes, moist with tears, were focused on him and him alone. Herb looked back with his tired eyes that spoke the message of time slipping quickly.

As I walked in, I spoke quietly. "Hi. I am Chaplain Jack, and I got here as quickly as I could."

"Thank you for coming so quickly, Chaplain," a voice from the kitchen rang out. I turned to see a younger woman that I assumed was the daughter. In complete defiance of the situation, Molly's smile was warm and alive. "My favorite godfather is having a tough time today."

"He is my angel, my strong man." Annie spoke and turned to me with a gracious and accepting smile. Her face was one that time had wonderfully sculpted from a gorgeous youth, to a gorgeous age. It was filled with the lines of time, but not with distraction from her beauty; rather, it enhanced it somehow. "Welcome, Chaplain Jack. This is my Herbert, my life for these last sixty-seven years."

I warmly took her hand, and then bent down to Herb. "Herb, you have quite an admiration club here. You must have done something right in your life."

Herb, despite the cancer tearing at his very breath, smiled at me and said, "They never really knew me."

It was incomprehensible to me that one so close to death could still joke, and be present to this moment with the ones he loved. But joke he did. And then as if passing to a different place, he closed his eyes and winced. The nurse quickly came to his side and said, "Herb, take this." She placed the morphine from the dropper under his tongue with a care, precision, and gentleness that only comes with experience and a big heart.

Herb accepted the drops, and looked out from his tired eyes once more. I knelt next to him, and Annie joined me, sitting and holding his hand, and she began to speak of a life of sixty-seven years. There was the meeting at the church, the trance she was in as she looked at him in his uniform, the dating that lasted through college and war, and finally their wedding day some sixty-three years ago last month. Herb was her life. God did not grant them children, and that great disappointment was somewhat tempered by good friends, good times, and a goddaughter named Molly, who stood at the side of the bed, with quiet admiration for a story told several hundred times to her that forever gets better with each telling.

Herb quietly slept while the story of their lives rolled out to me. His breathing was irregular and measured. This story of Annie and Herb was about to have another chapter written, the last chapter.

As Herb slept, it became apparent that the end was not as imminent, as suddenly his eyes popped open and gazed straight at me. "How about a little pudding?" Annie asked. His eyes went back to that familiar gaze. He nodded and agreed, probably more out of habit than desire. "Pudding is all he has eaten for the last week," Annie said, as she scooted across the room to the kitchen.

Returning to the living room, she spooned out the pudding to Herb with a delicate touch that spoke of an artist. Each extra smidge of pudding was removed. After two bites, Herb nodded *enough*, and spoke softly, "I want to sleep some more, sweetie."

She nodded, stopped, and handed the pudding offering to Molly. Annie then kissed her knight gently on the cheek. "Sleep." As Herb closed his eyes, Annie's eyes filled with tears that streamed down the gentle wrinkles provided by time.

I prayed, but remember not the words. I called upon a loving God to provide the right moment of death, and provide the peace we all needed at the time. As too often happens when I pray in these situations, I open my eyes to people crying, and all except Herb, had tears.

Herb lived on that morning into the afternoon. Strangely, we shared talk, a piece of chocolate pie that Annie had made two days ago, and memories, as Herb slowly moved toward that ultimate moment that punctuates life.

When the moment finally came, Herb's breath decreased and then just stopped. Annie held him, kissing him on his forehead, with a repeated phrase whispered only for him. Herb died in the arms of the woman he loved; there is no better way to die. Connected.

The after-death minutes that seem like almost an eternity. Annie and Molly sobbed. We held them, prayed with them, and allowed the time to be theirs. But then the time of death becomes a task of "now what?" We at hospice have learned to handle these moments the best we can, usually with grace.

The funeral home was called, and the time came to have Herb go from their home. The nurse suggested that I move Annie into the other room as she prepared Herb to leave.

We went into the other room. This woman of eighty-eight years was crying, but also thankful that Herb, her man, had died the way he wanted to, at home, with her and Molly. We spoke of that gift. I told her that the next few minutes, when Herb's body was being removed, would be hard. She looked at me and went silent. After a minute or two, she asked me a question. "Chaplain Jack, tell me. Will I get to see him again?"

As an ordained minister, you study theology and scripture, you pray, you write, you contemplate, you meditate. With all the study and time, when such a question is posed to you at such a meaningful moment, you never can respond with a formulated response, or with a perfect quote. What comes out is not a refined theology, not a treatise on life after death, or the cross and the resurrection. What comes out is what you really believe in your heart and gut.

Without hesitation, I said, "Oh, yes, ma'am. You will see Herb again, when your time comes. Herb will be at the gates of Heaven, standing next to Jesus, motioning you to eternity. You will see him again. A love like you two share can never be destroyed." I believed that then, and I believe it now.

When we connect our hearts we attain something well beyond explanation. That uniting, that bond I believe is of God, in fact is God. The connection that Annie and Herb had was life giving, sustaining, supporting. It bonded and gave purpose and unity in their life. Did it elongate their lives together, I do not know. But the sixty-seven years they shared were life giving to each other. They enjoyed their lives, suffered the disappointment of not having children, but connections to their faith communities and goddaughter gave their life a taste and flavor that was rich.

Connection is life giving for those that I come in contact with. Connection can be in a profound way between two people like Annie and Herb, or it can be in community of friends. As I show in this next story.

Connection

How much do you have?

*Pale Death with impartial tread beats at
the poor man's cottage door and at the pal-
aces of kings.*

Horace (65 BC–8 BC), Odes

Occasionally, I would be on twenty-four-hour duty
at the hospital. It was typical to have numerous
death calls. In a large metropolitan area, it was not
unusual to have people die on emergency calls at the
hospital. I got a call one night that amazed me as I
saw the way in which connection works amongst the
poor of the city.

Hazel had died of a heart attack. Hazel was
eighty-three and had a history of heart disease, so
this was not an unexpected event at all. I checked at
the emergency room desk before I went to the room.
Hazel's daughter and granddaughter had arrived
and were in the waiting room. They had followed
the ambulance, but had not heard that Hazel had
not made it.

I went with the doctor, who explained the sad
news. The daughter Ruth was not shocked, just
looked at me. Jessha, the granddaughter, started to
sob. These people were poor, from their dress, the
resignation in their reaction. Ruth said, "I knew

Momma wasn't going to make it. She'd been too sick, too long." Jessha cried on, not in wailing which happens sometimes with an African American family.

I took them to see Hazel. We spoke, prayed, tears flowed, and tenderness was expressed.

The family and friends gathered in the chapel, I offered a prayer, which was accepted and acknowledged. Then Hazel's neighbor Ruby said, "Well if Hazel gonna get buried, I guess we better make some arrangements." She then surveyed the room, with a deep profound knowing of the circumstances, and she grabbed the phone. The voices offered funeral homes, the debate settled on one, and a call was made. "Gonna cost $1,250," she exclaimed as she put down the phone.

"Sounds okay." Jessha spoke, while still dabbing her eyes with the Kleenex I had brought.

Ruby looked out, opened her purse, and said, "I got $150." She looked at everyone. "How much do you have?" As in a magnificent cathedral, with gold laid baskets, each looked into their purse and wallets. Each smart enough to have their money always with them. Each digging into a reserve that was no reserve. It was the multiplication of loaves and fishes amongst poor folk.

With $537 that Ruth had stuck away for Hazel's care if she had to go to a home, the money was going to be available. This web of women pieced together a connection to bury their friend, mother, aunt, and sister. She was going to get a proper burial.

I am sometimes amazed at the poor. They have a community of themselves that sustains life and supports each other. This is the web of connection that, if only could be imitated in government or churches, would provide a powerful presence. This I believe is exactly what the early Christians experienced when it says in Acts 2:44, 45: "All who believed were together and had all things in common: they would sell their possessions and goods and distribute the proceeds to all, as any had need."

Each of the women, with virtually nothing, knew in their "web" that all things were held in common, and as the need arose, the distribution would be done, even in Hazel's death. We live in a culture, a society in the United States, that laughs at this type of charity and commonality. But I wonder, is this not what we seek? We seek a deep "connectiveness" that unites us, not separates us. I think this is a foundation of the "Reign of God" in our midst. This indeed is the loaves and fishes.

I have had the wonderful opportunity to be part of two men's Bible studies. These have both been in communities that are in the upper socio-economic status. One of the neat things that one of the groups started was that each week when we came we would throw a dollar or so in a five-gallon water jug, and at the end of the year we would use the money to repair bicycles or buy toys for the poor. One session we met that spoke volumes about the concept of connection.

Connection

Sharing a Bottle at Christmas

"Any other commandment, are summed up in this word, "Love your neighbor as yourself."

Romans 13:9 (NRSV)

I sat next to Dan quite by accident, or so I thought. The Bible study group was large this week, probably around thirty-five or so. I don't remember the scripture exactly, but we were a few days or so from Christmas. About twenty-five minutes into the reflection and sharing, I noticed that Dan was crying. Although there were times when tears were shed during our men's Bible study, it certainly was the odd occasion when that occurred. Dan was a very sensitive man, with a huge heart, a deep love of God, and a deep connection to all he met, and especially with his family.

I noticed the tears, and did not want to embarrass Dan, so I quietly placed my hand on his shoulder, leaned close, and asked, "You okay?" Dan nodded *yes* with his head, but with the shoulders sunk, a deeply sad and troubled face, I knew this was a lie. The tears no longer were isolated, but had turned into a stream down this fine man's cheeks.

Meanwhile, the group had gone off into a loud discussion, where someone was being good-naturedly teased, and the din of the group disguised our little discussion. I reached around Dan with my arm and held him, and Dan began to sob.

As one noticed, then another, the loud din faded into deep silence. I said, " I think our brother is hurting." Dan, with enormous emotion, attempted several times to control his sobs, without a great deal of success. The rest of the group sat with anticipation, wonder, and fear as they experienced the rawness of hurt pouring out from our friend.

Dan finally mustered the courage and found a place where he could speak. "You see, I do not know what to do. I have this one job, and one of my guys cut the marble wrong, and it had to be replaced. That was well over two thousand dollars that I just don't have. I told the people I was doing the job for that I would make it right, but the money I had to use was the money for our house payment, and …"

Dan had started his business about a year ago, and we all knew it was not easy or going all that well. Kitchen cabinets were always in demand, but it was a hard business. Dan continued, "I don't know how it happened, we are back about two months on our house, there is enough money in this job, but I have to have it done by next Wednesday, or I will forfeit it all …" Silence absorbed us all and covered us like a cloak. We sat in rapt attention as if the Lord himself were speaking to us. And maybe he was.

As Dan finally regained his composure, his story went to the lack of Christmas for his five kids, the knowledge that he had extended too far. "I prayed last night for some type of miracle. Maybe God is telling me something, maybe my pride is too great. What am I to do?"

"What is left to be done on the job?" The question came from Don.

"How much do you need?" from Jim.

"I have some tools."

"We could ..." The silence broke into questions, suggestions, and evolved to a plan. It would require some days of sacrifice by many in that group.

I asked, "Who has the bottle? Pass it around to me." As it passed, like a collection basket, each wallet opened, and to all the dollars that were there, more bills floated into the bottom. One counted the bottle. "We have $893!"

This money would cover Dan's house payment. We prayed over Dan and extended our lives into his.

It was midnight mass, and Dan and his wife and kids arrived, and I greeted them just before the mass started. His eyes were moist again. The job got done, the Christ child was born in his life, and the echoes of Mary when she heard of her responsibility in the life's of this world when she said "My soul magnifies the Lord ... His mercy is for those that fear him ... (he) has lifted up the lowly, he has filled the hungry with great things" (Luke 1:47, 52b-53 NRSV). The words of Zechariah (Luke 1:78–79 NRSV) that were proclaimed that night found a wonderful newness into my heart as I looked upon Dan and his family as they came forward to receive communion, "By the tender mercy of our God the dawn from on high will break upon us, to give light to those in darkness and in the shadow of death, to guide our feet into the way of peace."

As Gunderson and Pray say in their book, connection is "the web of relationships that nurture, sustain, and serve as a source of healing; the social fabric of person's lives" (Gunderson, Insert). In the story of Hazel as well as the story of Dan, the key to our living is in our connectedness to one another.

We live out the reality of Jesus' presence if only we see his face in those around us, and act as if our connectedness is there. In a world of individualism, which is pounded into us through the media, we must connect to find wholeness through each other and through our God, living as the body of Christ. This connectedness does sustain and provide.

Now what happens, if it is not present.

Connection

I don't want you here!

I'd rather get my brains blown out in the wild than wait in terror at the slaughterhouse.

Craig Volk, *Northern Exposure*,
"A Hunting We Will Go," 1991.

When I walked into the hospital room, the woman in the bed was quiet; her eyes were closed, and seemed to be peaceful, but not necessarily at sleep.

"Ms. Leary?" I inquired.

"Yes," she responded, opening her eyes and focusing on me.

"I am Chaplain Jack. Do you have some time for a visit with me?"

"Sure," she welcomed, "I'd like that."

In the next hour, we spoke of her tumor, which was ravaging her abdomen and refusing to leave, laying claim to her life. We spoke of her boyfriend that she had been living with for the last two years, who had helped her get along for the last few months, once she had stopped working. We spoke of the unfortunate reality that she would have to go and live with her mother, who Gerri Leary did not want to live with.

We spoke of the years of sadness when Gerri was young, of the tortured years of mother's endless demands upon her, which Gerri felt she could never live up to. The hurt turned to tears, which became quiet rage and anger within this woman who lay in the bed with a tumor growing.

We spoke of other ways she could survive for the time she had left, but it did come out that this boyfriend had kind of disappeared from her life in the last few weeks. The regular visits became irregular, and had turned into no visits for the last five days, and the phone was no longer being answered.

This fragile woman, strong in her nature and resolve but deeply weak in body, had no alternatives. The only remaining place was her mother's home.

We prayed that day together, prayed for peace in her relationships, some peaceful connection that would sustain her. Gerri was a troubled person, of that it was certain, and her journey toward death would be a difficult one, I sensed. I prayed as I walked away that somehow, that connection we had made in the hospital room could be used in the future.

It was a few weeks later, and the call came in from Gerri's mother, Mrs. Woods, pleading with me to come and see Gerri. Mrs. Woods was deeply concerned for her daughter, not only for her physical condition that was worsening, but also for her spiritual wellbeing, and, as Mrs. Woods, described it, "I fear for her soul, Chaplain. Please come."

I explained that I had attempted to visit several times, but was always told "not today" by Gerri. I had spoken to her nurse Pam, and she said Gerri had isolated herself in the basement of the home, rarely accepted her mother into the room, and only she and the nursing assistant had visited in the last couple of weeks. Pam said that she knew Gerri would benefit from my visit, and she would talk to her.

Pam did talk with Gerri and told me that she agreed to have me come. I attempted to call her prior to my visit with the nurse, but never had a response. The nurse assured me it would be okay, and that she would be with her when I arrived. Pam told me that Gerri had expressed trust in no one, especially God, but that she had remembered me in the hospital and thought it would be all right if I came.

As I came into the room, the bed was in the center of the large basement bedroom. Gerri lay in the bed, with a fairly distended stomach, as that tumor had laid claim to a residence that would soon be destroyed by its very occupation. I approached through the door, with Gerri looking away from my entrance, staring at the big screen that had been placed so that she could watch TV. Pam was there with what looked as a fearful look, which I interpreted as concern, as I knew Gerri was progressing fast.

"Hi, Gerri. It's Chaplain Jack."

"What the hell are you doing here? I don't want you here! Get out." Her eyes had fury as she stared at Pam.

Pam said, "Remember, we talked about having the chaplain come and see you."

"Get out of here, now," she screamed.

"No problem, sorry for the misunderstanding," I quietly said, hiding my pounding heart with the rough rebuff.

I left the basement, returned to my car, got back on the road, and prayed.

My phone went off a few minutes later. It was Pam. "I am so sorry Jack. She just flipped on me." I told her it wasn't her fault, and that I was going to be fine, it was all part of my job. We spoke of Gerri, her status, and the troubled state of affairs in that home.

Gerri died one week later and had no funeral.

The missing of connection in our lives is a lonely place. I am not sure that Gerri did not have a deep psychological problem that plagued her. I have no real knowledge of her family history or her private life. I only had a small amount of bits and pieces of a very complex puzzle of her life.

I do know that any connection in life, family, communities, church, or work all seemed to be missing in her life. I was thankful that Gerri had Pam. Pam was her sole connection, the best I could understand. Isolation is a serious condition that does not cause life. But even if we are not connected, due to circumstances beyond our control sometimes, does not mean that connection can occur.

My last story on connection is one that was told to me by a dear man, Wayne, who has since passed on to his own reward with God. His story spoke to me of the power of connection. It was his story, and I relate it to you in honor of his memory. It was transformative to Wayne, and that is one great benefit of connection.

Connection

Thank You

I hope the leaving is joyful.

– Frida Kahlo

Wayne seemed uneasy as he looked at us in the Clinical Pastoral Education Group after sharing one of his recent visits with a patient. His discussion was well done, but yet it seemed as if he had something else on his mind.

Finally, after a long bit of silence, Wayne took a deep breath and sighed. He finally spoke. "I really wanted to share a different experience with you, rather than the one I shared … but I was afraid that you would think I was crazy." After some quiet reassurance and nods from his group, he started.

"I was on call at the hospital last weekend. My beeper went off, and the nurse asked me if I could come up and spend some time with a patient that was nearing death. It was in the neurology ICU. This patient, as the nurse explained, had been comatose with a brain tumor for months, her vital signs were dropping, and the nearest relatives, although they had been called, were in Texas. The nurse thought it would be nice if someone was, well, just with her for a while.

"So, I went up to the floor, and just as the nurse had said this lady, Mrs. Friend, was indeed comatose, and based on her breathing was getting close. She wasn't frail as so many people are as they near death. In fact, she looked physically to be okay. She was a bit older than me. She had gray hair tied back, and had a pleasant enough face. She looked sad, though. I wasn't able to understand how someone who had been comatose for as long as she had been could express something like that. I figured I was just imagining it. As I would always do, I decided to read some scripture to her, and then something told me to pray. My prayer was a deep one that really came from my heart in a way that was more than it sometimes usually is, I am not sure why. I asked God on her behalf to give his mercy, and love to this woman…just as I was concluding, my beeper went off. It was the ER, and I finished my prayer and left.

"Something told me after the hour I spent with another family to return to Mrs. Friend. When I arrived at the nurse's station, the nurse I had talked to before said that Mrs. Friend had passed about ten minutes before. I was not shocked but felt sad that I could not have been there with her at that last moment, especially because of the deep prayer that I had gone to in her presence. I told the nurse that I was going to go in and pray for her a bit longer. As I went, in the nurse closed the drapes around the bed, and the door behind us.

"I looked at Mrs. Friend. The breathing was gone, but I noticed that the sadness had also disappeared from her face. I kneeled down next to the bed and began to pray for her, and strangely returned to that same depth of prayer where I had left off. It was then that I felt someone sitting on the bed next to me. I had not heard anyone come in. Was it the nurse, or the doctor? I opened by eyes, and there was Mrs. Friend, smiling, looking down at me in the dusk of the room. She seemed very alive. Her face was somehow different though, her eyes were calm and at peace. She spoke to me. 'Thank you. Thank you, Wayne, for spending my last moments on earth with me. I was glad to not be alone. Thank you for being with me.' With that she smiled. I did not know if I was startled, in shock, or in a trance. But she seemed very real. I got up went to the nurse and asked her to check Mrs. Friend one more time. The nurse stared at me, then assured me that Mrs. Friend was quite gone. I asked quietly, with my heart pounding furiously, please. With that the nurse went in, and verified that Mrs. Friend had passed away."

Wayne said he stood there, said thanks, and left, unsure as to how to explain what had happened, or even if it happened. We all sat in rapt silence, listening to Wayne as tears streamed from his eyes.

He finally said, "Thank you for hearing this. I knew that you could hear it. I know she visited me and said thank you."

Wayne died just two months later of a massive coronary, all alone.

The power of connection is one that we can never really understand. All I know is that it is important and has great meaning for life. Our need as humans, as children of God, is to be connected once again to our source, and we do it on this planet, it seems, one brother and sister at a time.

Every time I go and visit a patient who is non-responsive or in a coma, I remember Wayne, Mrs. Friend, and know that communication and connection is not all auditory, but is very deeply spiritual. You just never know how we touch each other in this web of relationships.

It seems odd, from a story that seems impossible to move toward the idea of coherence, but life does hinge on making sense of our lives, in ways that seem on the surface as very incoherent, almost nonsense. Finding a way to add meaning to our life's events has been going on. Just ask all of those that wrote the scriptures.

COHERENCE

COHERENCE: Meaning and belonging, "…a master narrative held so deeply that it goes beneath language and into consciousness…an assumption that life holds together in the face of the most difficult and horrible circumstances."

What happens to us on this planet seems grossly unfair, unpredictable, and out of our control. But somehow we have a deep need to have meaning to what we do, what happens to us, who we are in this vastness of the universe. If not, I suspect we all might just wander around in an endless mix of lust, grief, and hunger, and never be able to see beauty in anything. As Wally "Famous" Amos said, "Life is just a mirror, and what you see out there, you must first see inside of you."

Father Richard Rohr, a Franciscan priest, said that he encountered a monk on the road on the way back from a monastery. These monks were sworn to silence, but this aged monk stopped him and said, "You are Father Richard, are you not, and you get to preach and speak?"

Father Richard said, "Yes, I do."

"Then tell them all this: 'God is not out there.'" With that, the monk went on his way.

After years of prayer, study, and devotion to an invisible God, his key meaning in life came to be God is not out there. So let's look at stories where that search for meaning and belonging live, or does not live.

Coherence

Just not Today

For certain is death for the born
And certain is birth for the dead;
Therefore over the inevitable
Thou shouldst not grieve.

Bhagavad Gita (250 BC–250 AD)

"That's right, it's all gonna work out in God's good time." Those were the first words I ever heard from Aneda Smith. This ninety-four-year-old, African American survivor.

I have had the extraordinary privilege of knowing extraordinary people in my life. My mother was such a person; she had strength and resilience inside of her that I could watch her tap that seemed almost limitless. I have known great teachers whose love for their topic and love for their students were so interwoven that it flowed like a river. I have known great women and men of faith. They were wonderful examples of dedication and faith.

But one person that stands out more than almost all the rest is Ms. Smith. Ms. Aneda Smith was one of my hospice patients who was diagnosed with lung cancer, congestive heart failure, and a host of other deadly diagnoses, some four years from the time in which I last visited her. This is one of those women that as her story has unfolded to me, I stand more and more in awe and wonder.

A native to Memphis, with seven children, three of which she had buried now. She buried her husband. She was raised on a farm as a youth, with her Daddy as a sharecropper. We shared many wonderful afternoons sitting on her couch, talking of life, talking of family, talking of God, and talking of death.

Ms. Smith had a quality about her, where I knew I sat at the foot of wisdom. She had a smile and chuckle that would warm the coldest of hearts. She would listen deeply to all that you said, comment if appropriate, and offer perspective that only came from a life lived with reverence for a God that could be trusted, and hence a life that could be trusted.

Ms. Smith welcomed strangers, welcomed the hurting, and cared deeply for so many. Loved her little grandson, that I became great friends with at her home. She, at the age of ninety-four, was still the captain of the local Neighborhood Watch, and attended every event at her church that she had attended for well over fifty years. She loved with a deep heart. She is the person closest to Jesus' description of what the disciples were to be like, lambs amongst the wolves. She was a lamb, but wily. A founding member of the NAACP in Memphis, and at each of her birthday parties, she had mayors, senators, and the leaders of all key organizations in the city. She lamented over her city and what had happened. I would seek her out on her thoughts on violence, war, and race relations. Always prophetic, always in step with her Lord.

One day, Ms. Smith told me of her daily prayer. "Oh Lord, I know that you will decide on which day I will die, and I accept that, but just not today." How much longer she will live indeed is up to her and God, and I believe God will have to tell her to come, and she will obey on that day.

She told me of the day that Reverend Martin Luther King Jr. was assassinated. Told me of the horror and sadness, and rage that gripped this city. "The main thing I remember was that I knew inside that we all had to go on, that Martin had done what he needed to do, and we had to keep carrying on, and do our part. I have tried to hold up my part of the bargain."

Ms. Smith is still alive and still looking to God, as of this writing. And when she does pass she will pass with few regrets but a marvelous legacy.

In the definition of coherence is the phrase, "...a master narrative held so deeply that it goes beneath language and into consciousness...an assumption that life holds together in the face of the most difficult and horrible circumstances." That is who Ms. Smith is to me. Facing the death of children, death in the civil rights movement, she always sought out the "holding together of it all," some way, some how.

She saw no color on my face, she only saw my heart and what it held. Is that not coherence in life? What is it that we hold on to that allows us this Cause of Life or allows us not to have it? Let's discuss one who had the coherence, just never could quite grasp it.

Coherence

Why won't he let me die?

*Life is pleasant. Death is peaceful. It's the
transition that is troublesome.*

Isaac Asimov

It had been four weeks since the crisis, when we
thought Leona was going to die that day. Somehow the chariot that was supposed to come missed
Leona's daughter's house, where she now lived. She
did not die, her breathing decreased, blood pressure
dropped, tears were shed, and her husband Hank
almost went into cardiac arrest himself that day. But
she came back. The stroke's effect took a step back
from the edge of the cliff, and once again, Leona was
suffering through each day.

I had visited her and Hank a few weeks prior,
and was still concerned at that time that she might
relapse. On this visit, according to the nurses who
said she was doing "much better," weak but better, I
needed as chaplain to take a different tact. She was
not going to die, at least not soon; how does life,
unexpected and perhaps even unwanted, get lived?

As I entered the room, with Hank in his easy
chair at the foot of Leona's bed, just as I had left
him two weeks ago. Leona was propped up by a pil-

low, her face, as usual, ashen, her breathing and spirit weak, but she was stable and would live for a while.

"Hi, Hank," I said as I shook his hand. "Hi, Ms. Leona. How are you feeling?"

As Leona opened her mouth, Hank spoke for her, as he normally did, "Well, she is not doing so good today, but I guess it is as good as can be expected." Leona rolled her eyes in frustration, with Hank, with his poor hearing, always putting words in her mouth.

"I guess I am glad to hear that. But what about you, Ms. Leona?" I tried once more, leaning in toward Leona in the bed, pulling up my chair.

"Not very good, Chaplain. I don't know why he (God) wants me to live. I pray every night that he will take me. It is as if he cannot hear my prayer. Why won't he let me die?" Leona rasped out, in the tiny voice that was left to her.

"Well, Leona, God must have a purpose for you to live on this way. I may never fully understand it, but you are here, and may be for some time. I think there is purpose here that we may never be privy to. I guess we are stuck with you for a while."

This brought a chuckle out of Leona, and she said, "Yeah, I guess you are stuck with me, aren't you?"

"Are you eating much?" I asked.

"I have no taste for food, but Hank makes me eat."

Hank injected, "We try to get her up and eat with us. I hope she can get better soon." Now Leona had almost died twice in the last three months, but Hank had denial down fairly well as a mode of coping.

It was interesting to watch the two of them bicker and banter back and forth. Something learned in their sixty-three years of marriage. There was much unspoken love, not much spoken though. Each time we would pray, Hank and Leona would cry, Leona sometimes with a wailing sob in anguish. The reality they were living on this deathwatch came to light for them only in prayer. Leona sick, Hank not much better, dreaming of return to their farm up north where they had made their lives together for so long.

"Tell me, Leona, why do you think God does not grant you your desire and prayer to die?" I asked, not understanding it myself, as I watched this seventy-pound shell of the woman she once was struggle on.

"I wish I knew, but I just don't. I just want the Good Lord to take me." A simple request denied.

"Would you like for me to pray for your death?" A dumb question by me.

"Yes."

We prayed together, Leona, Hank, and I, for death to come that day. Hank did not like it, and I could feel it in his hands as he squeezed my hand, as I asked for God's mercy not to prolong the suffering of Leona. He knew, she knew, I knew, and God knew the desire. This long suffering makes no sense. The tears came to us all. Sadness, not for her illness, but for the loss of understanding on all of our parts.

As I reached for the door, after saying the prayer, and attempting to put a bit of hope back into their deathwatch, I heard Leona say in her whispery voice.

"Thank you, Chaplain. I do not know what we would do without you."

As I left that day, I did not feel that I had been any help at all to one who wanted to die.

Leona passed in my presence two months later, very peacefully. I held Hank in my arms as he wept. His wish had not been granted, but her prayer finally was. We may never know why she was alive and suffered for the two to three extra months. I personally am not sure that it matters that we do know how it fits together.

To Leona, life in the last six months had lost meaning, lost coherence. It had gone on a bit too long. All the dreams they once lived, shared on their farm had vanished. Hank held onto a thread of hope for a miraculous healing, but it, like death, was not meant to be a beckoned visitor to Leona.

There are times in each of our lives where coherence is lost. Our simple handhold on reality slips away from us, and we are plunged into wonder, doubt, and mystery. Coherence as a cause for living becomes an illusion that eludes us. It is part of the strange way in which our lives go on, some too short, some too long.

Whatever the reason, our search for coherence, meaning, and belonging is part of our life's journey. In this next story I tell the story of a man, who after fifty-plus years of holding on to something, put a past event back into a perspective he could live with, and found coherence that had been lost in one part of his life.

Coherence

And I did nothing

*The Dead cannot cry out for justice; it is
the duty of the living to do so for them.*

Lois McMaster Bujold,
Diplomatic Immunity, 2002

It was a dark and overcast day when I went to visit
Mr. Bellow. I had always enjoyed my visits with him
over the last four months. He always welcomed me,
and his daughter said that he spoke often about our
visits, and she believed that he told me things that he
had not told to others. I was a bit concerned about
him, for the nurse had said that he was starting to
show some significant signs of failure.

It was late in the afternoon, and what little light
was coming in the window backlit this fragile little
man. He always showed a friendly face and a wide
smile with his dentures in position. It was hard to see
his face this day, with the dim little side lamp that
was next to his chair, and the way the light played in
the room. I did not sense a smile.

I sat across from him, and his daughter excused
herself, as was her custom to give us privacy.

Over the months, Mr. Bellow had told me tales of
his life, from being involved in the building of dams
on the Kentucky and Tennessee Rivers to serving in

World War II. He fought at the Battle of the Bulge, one of the bloodiest in the history of the world. He was an interesting man, small of stature, but he had a big heart, a sense of adventure, and a genuine love of God.

He wasted no time today; the pleasantries were not deemed necessary.

"Chaplain, I need to tell you something," he started, peering upward from a bowed sitting position. "Do you remember me telling you that I served in Europe during the war?"

"I do, and I remember you saying you were in the Battle of the Bulge," I offered.

"I have been thinking and praying hard about those memories, and that is what I want to talk to you about. You see, I was a clerk to a colonel in the Army at the time, his adjunct. I handled all his papers and stuff. But at that battle there was little paperwork, because everyone had to fight. Night and day the battle went on. The sounds, the blood, the death was just overwhelming. You never knew from one moment to the other whether you would be wiped out by a shell, or tanks, or a sniper. It was as close to that place called hell as I ever want to get.

"One of the things that the Germans did was to drop paratroopers behind the lines, dressed as American soldiers. They spoke perfect English, and you could not tell them from the regular GIs. We hated them. They would direct our troops into ambushes. It happened a lot.

"Well, one day we caught seven of them. We were all so happy. They were paraded right through our camp. The colonel came to me and said he had to talk to me. Since I kept the records, I had to document all the comings and goings of prisoners. He told me that they were going to take those Germans out to the field and kill them. He said, 'Let our boys do what they needed to do.' I just stared at him. It was hell out there, but we had never done this to a prisoner, not that I knew of. I just stared. He looked straight at me, and said, 'Any questions?' I said, 'No, sir.'

"The prisoners and a group of the soldiers went off. I heard some screams, some howls, some cries that haunt me even today, and then a lot more than seven bullets. I filed no paperwork on them.

"And as I have thought about this …"

Mr. Bellow started to cry, which turned into sobs, and then almost wails of anguish.

"And I did nothing." I reached over, held this sad little soldier in my arms, and let him cry. Finally, the sobs stopped; I handed him a Kleenex.

He looked up at me and said, "Can God, any God, ever forgive this?"

After several moments, I just said, "Yes, I believe that God is of infinite mercy. It was what Jesus was born, lived, and died for. That is what I believe."

Finally, after many moments of silence, this little proud soldier mustered up enough courage to make his shoulders align. Then he looked and said, "I am deeply tired. Would you mind if I got some sleep?"

"Not at all." I said a prayer of seeking of forgiveness for all of us. I left, and he slept.

Two days later, he lapsed into unconsciousness, and a week later his cancer took his life.

War is a corporate sin. It ravages souls, brings us to a place of survival, hatred, and despair. Victory is an illusion. It only is a declaration of a time of war that has passed. Who won is irrelevant, who lost, who bears the incoherence of war and killing other humans, is the real defeat, the legacy of tragedy that tears at souls.

Mr. Bellow died, I believe, in peace, forgiven.

Having coherence, meaning, and belonging in life goes beyond taking care of the buddy in the foxhole. It can never be reduced to just that. These soldiers bear not only the price of the horror, they bear the memories, the sights, and the sounds for all of their lives, and from what I have seen and heard, takes great attack at all the causes of life.

But forgiveness, deep and real soul-searching forgiveness, can bring back coherence. It did for my friend Mr. Bellow.

And now for a quick story about a remarkable man, and the lucky stick.

Coherence

The Walking Stick

The secret of a good life is to have the right loyalties and hold them in the right scale of values.

Norman Thomas

Lars was a tall man. Must have been six-foot-five at least. He had that Scandinavian look to him–a shock of blond hair, a rather set jaw, and thin stature. This part due to his heritage, part due to his pancreatic cancer that was large, growing, and deadly. Lars would not last another week, two at the most, and he knew it.

In the other room was his wife of fifty-four years, who too would be dying shortly. She suffered from a series of mental disorders. But Lars loved Shirley. He explained that she had not had any serious debilitation until the last five years. She sensed Lars was dying, but when he was with her, he never let on that he was sick. He treated her with respect, love, caring, and compassion. In the ten minutes that we sat there, while this couple shared their lunch, he cared for her, when it was obvious that the very sight of food made him nauseous. She never spoke, just stared, and occasionally would moan.

How does one make sense of life, when so much seems wrong? A mentally and physically ill wife, a cancer ready to be succumbed to, a life that was to be gone well too soon, with an extremely shortened "happy" time. But I sensed no bitterness in Lars; in fact, I sensed he was indeed a happy man.

He, with the help of his granddaughter Mona, got Ms. Shirley into bed, and we got to talk a bit. He told me of his life, his loves, his inventions, his family, his work, his boat, and his faith. He loved his God, and loved his God through all his other loves. He was loyal, faithful, and had a knowledge and wisdom that was profound. We sat and shared for over an hour, or rather, he talked, and I listened.

With a twinkle in his eyes, he told me of his encounter with God. "I was about forty or so, had eight kids, a demanding business, and it was when I first sensed that Shirley was seriously mentally ill. It was crushing me. We were devoted to our faith, went to church, but so many things were wrong. I sat quietly one day, after mass, in the back of the church, praying. I had just been to my Cursillo retreat. It was a great retreat for me. I felt God's love for me deeply and personally. But when I came back, all my problems were still there. And I almost felt the need to lapse back into despair that I had before the retreat."

He adjusted his position, as it seemed as if the cancer was striking another right cross to him. I asked, "Are you okay, Lars?" He smiled at me.

"No, it hurts, but it will pass." He continued, "So I sat there, looking at my hands, and I glanced up at the crucifix, way up in the front of the church. Jesus hung there. And I knew at that moment, as a peace flooded over me, that I never had to be alone in my life and that my problems were always going to be shared. That man that hung there was going to be with me, forever. I knew it.

"Whether Shirley got better or worse, whether the business succeeded or failed, I would never be alone. I felt lucky and blessed, and decided or was assured at that moment, that I was the luckiest man ever made. I have had the happiest life, since that moment. I am blessed."

I just stared, then smiled. I have had my share of difficulties and tragedies in life, and too often can lapse into good old-fashioned "self pity." Lars had somehow mastered that, found the peace that surpasses all understanding, as St. Paul said in Philippians.

"Chaplain, let me give you something." Lars stood up, crossed the room, and in the corner picked up a walking stick. He returned to me and looked at it, held it in his two massive hands, and said, "This is a lucky walking stick, made from a beaver that gnawed the bark off of it for lunch one day. The Native Americans always thought it lucky to find and have one of these. Here." Lars extended it too me.

"It works, you know," he said as I twirled it in my hands.

"It does?" said I, the unbeliever.

"Yep, don't you believe it?" Then his eyebrows went up as his gaze pierced my unbelieving eyes and soul. "Had any bad luck since you have had it?" With that this large man, with the large hands and large spirit, let out a great laugh, and I, the unbeliever, stood transformed to a believer.

This man, looking down the short barrel of deadly gun called pancreatic cancer. This man, with a wife, sick and not able to comprehend that her husband was dying. This man, large of stature and large of heart, had a deep sense of reality and life, and shared it with me, the supposed man of God.

The next time I saw Lars was six days later, unconscious, lying in bed, a few hours from death. We gathered the family, including Shirley, around his deathbed, and we prayed for my friend Lars. As the prayer concluded, before I could utter the conclusion, Shirley said, "Amen." All were shocked, for she had not spoken in years. Shirley turned, and with the aid of her daughter, went back to her bed. Lars died that afternoon.

To this day, I do not know if Lars was teasing me, playing a joke on me, or bestowing a great gift to me that day. But it will be a treasure to me the rest of my life, a constant reminder that indeed, I am a "lucky" man.

Coherence in life comes to us in strange ways. It is through our connection not only to people but also in our connection to the divine. It is that "master narrative held so deeply that it goes beneath language and into consciousness...an assumption that life holds together in the face of the most difficult and horrible circumstances" that is Gunderson and Pray's definition.

Lars had come to peace with life's strange and odd twists. Accepted them as part of life that surpasses our wildest understanding, and probably will not be understood fully.

We, as humans, can find so many things that just are not "sense making." We see tragedy and pain in so many in this world. We can easily slip out of the place where things all fit, for God's purposes, in ways not understandable. One of my favorite quotes is from Isaiah 55:8–11 (NRSV):

> For my thoughts are not your thoughts, nor are your ways my ways, says the Lord. For as the heavens are higher than the earth, so are my ways higher than your ways and my thoughts than your thoughts. For as the rain and the snow come down from heaven, and do not return there until they have watered the earth, making it bring forth and sprout, giving seed to the sower and bread to the eater, so

shall my word be that goes out from my mouth; it shall not return to me empty, but it shall accomplish that which I purpose, and succeed in the thing for which I sent it.

Coherence is different from understanding. It is more acceptance and the belief that life does hold together, for a purpose greater than we will ever be able to comprehend in this life at least.

Now let's talk of the innate ability to do what needs to be done, or Agency.

AGENCY

AGENCY: The capacity to act, "... a generative force that inevitably leads to the matter of call. It gives traction to three questions, 'What am I to do with my life? What have I been called to do? Am I doing it?'" Doing that goes beyond activity as such.

I discussed before the concept of Loss. Loss is of all the different ways in which we can know we are able to function and do in life. It is also the response to the questions posed by the definition used by Gunderson and Pray. Loss of life functionality, loss of abilities, loss of connection with family and friends, with church, with work all tax an individual. But it does not necessarily remove the desire to have Agency.

This is shown in my first example of an African American man, named Mr. Eddie Gerard.

Agency

My Daddy Taught Me

As men, we are all equal in the presence of death.

– Publius Syrus (ca. 100 BC)

I entered his nursing home room. He sat in the bed; it was obvious from his set jaw as I entered that he was pissed.

Mr. Gerard said, "Don' they know that they are takin' away my dignity? Hell, a man can't even get up and pee by himself. My daddy taught me never to back away from nobody, nobody, and now I can't even get up and pee. Hell. I'm sorry, Chaplain, but sittin' in this bed, and havin' to ring a bell to get someone to go pee, just ain't right.

"My daddy gave me the advice to never let anyone take advantage, no one. That as a black man we would have to stand up for ourselves, more so than any white man ever had to do. We could not let no one, no one, walk over us.

"There was the day when I was seven, and I wouldn't go around ole Boss Ames' leg when I was walkin' in front of the post office. He screamed at me, 'Boy, get back here!' I just turned and stared at him and walked away. My uncle overheard him say to his buddies, no boy was goin' not get out of his way. My uncle and my daddy got some guns, and they fired some shots when they came lookin' for trouble that night. They didn't come back, no sir. That was what my daddy taught me. You gotta be willin' to fight for what's is right.

"I had a night club, a real fine one, Chaplain. Not too far from here. Ms. Donald rented it to me. It was her property. She could rent it all right to me. It was about 1973 or so ... well, ole Boss Simpson didn't like that a black man was going to run a club in that neighborhood. Every so often he would show up and give my folks there some crap. One day he showed up, and he was raisin' hell about the club, and he found out that I had a black waitress. He was furious. He got to threatenin' my people and all. I was in the back, and I walked out and told him that this was my club, and he had no right to be in here yellin' and carrying on. He told me to stop bringing my kind into the club, and that I had no business there. I reached for my .45 caliber pistol, pointed it at him, and said that I not only had the right, but I had justice right here and now, if he wanted it. He stopped yellin.' He said he would see me in court, because there were laws about this.

"He sued me, and Ms. Donald, for a violation of some code, I think he made up. As we were going up the long steps of the courthouse, there was ole' Boss Simpson with a bunch of his goons at the top stair. I headed up the steps, and I heard a call from old Ms. Donald, 'Hey, Eddie.' I saw this old lady strugglin' up the stairs, so I went back to help her and took her arm. As we were going up, she leaned over to me and said in my ear, 'Eddie, stay right with me as we go up.' I told her I would. She said, 'No, you don't understand, I got word that Simpson is going to grab you and lynch you. They want to haul you off before we get into court. But they won't try if you stay with me.'

"We walked past those SOBs that day, went into court. His case was thrown out by the judge, who told him that the days of his bullying were over. Yessir, we won that day, and I didn't get lynched. Of course, at least one of them would have died first."

Sometime in our life we make a decision about life, and what it takes to make it through. Some can view it as a cosmic struggle. But Eddie decided that it was about what was right, and that no matter what, he would never, ever back down from a fight. Death was not as bad as living in a world where his ability to do what was only right, to act, to live as a free and equal man.

Agency is that ability to respond to that which is deep inside of us, to act. Eddie's inability to get up and urinate by himself tugged deep on that desire to act, to do what he was "called to do." How much of his story was bravado, how much was recalled through the eyes of desired memory, I will never know. But this scrappy little black man had more grit, more determination that came from his deep pride of being a man. Even in preparing to die soon, he was not going to go easily.

Now, I'll tell the story of a man I never heard a word from.

Agency

The Fist

It is sad when our Daddies die, Makes us one less person inside.

Pamela Ribon,
Why Girls are Weird.

Mr. Whiteman was a frail whisper of what he once was. His daughter and two granddaughters told me of how strong and vital he once was. He lay there looking at them, largely unable to move. The oxygen feed through the canula hung lazily from his ear, off center as if he had a third nostril. Gena, the blond granddaughter, adjusted it and poked her grandfather in the arm playfully.

His granddaughters teased with him. Mr. Whiteman, or "Bumps" as he was affectionately called, managed a smile as the two granddaughters took on a ritual that probably dated back to when they were kids. A version of "you always liked me best." This delighted Bumps. Although he had not voiced any words for over two weeks now, you could see in his eyes the joy these two brought to him. Their presence there was much more effective in bringing life to Bumps than the oxygen was at this point.

Bridget, the brunette-haired granddaughter, said, "Well, if you won't admit that I am your favorite then I am going to make you drink this Ensure that you don't like." With that a stirring occurred under the sheet. Somewhere deep in the memory, somewhere finding energy from an unknown source, slowly slipping out from the sheet, came the hand. This small, skin-on-bone hand emerged, and raised up. Where this man had been unable to do more than smile in the last three days, a hand emerged, pointed directly at Bridget and clenched into a fist. It then playfully waved at her.

Joyful giggles broke out; the women of Bumps' life had seen this many times before. Bumps' male act of defiance in the face of overwhelming female presence. The giggles matched the elation felt there that afternoon. Then the giggles were exposed by tears that ran down the cheeks of each of the women of Bumps' life. The fist slowly dropped down to his side. The hand was covered with the sheet again by Bridget, as Bumps took the opportunity to recover from this major exertion. Bumps slept, completely contented and loved.

I told this story at his funeral two weeks later, and the giggles and tears visited the family once more.

Agency is "the capacity to act." As we as people lose our capacity to act we grieve for each of our losses. Whether it is control over our sleeping, taking pills, rolling over, or raising a fist, each act and the capacity to do that act has profound meaning in our ability to have that "generative force."

In response to the question of what we are to do with the rest of our lives, we must come to the realization that as long as we have the capacity to act, we are alive and have that Agency that is life. Sometime it is in the fluttering of the eyelids, the stare at someone that we love, or a smile. Whatever it is, all of our acts have meaning and should be valued in what we do and what we say. No act is idle, and each act no matter how small answers the question posed, "Am I doing what I have been called to do?" The response of Bumps was what he was called to do, in response to love and a deep and wonderful relationship with his granddaughters.

But "acts" can also be for reasons that we may never understand, as is illustrated in this next story.

Agency

Why?

I guess that is how death works. It doesn't matter if we're ready or not. It just happens.

Randy K. Milholland,
Something Positive, 2006.

"I was up most of the night. His temperature jumped to 102 degrees at 2 a.m., and I thought that I had lost him, for sure. Do you want a cup of coffee?" Ellen asked.

"Thanks, Ellen, I think I will, I'll get it," I responded, as I looked in the sunken eyes of this woman, not that much younger than I was. I could not fathom how she was doing this; it had been almost a year and a half since Vince was diagnosed with his rare disease. A perfectly healthy young man, devoted to his mom, his faith, his God, his family, his friends. A superb student, a vibrant young man. He was the pride of his mom, the absolute apple of her eye.

Ellen was a living testimony to living on the edge of insanity and exhaustion. I was not sure if she would survive this if he lived much longer. The hospital in the apartment was replete with monitors, medical devices, shelves next to the bed where Vince lay, full of various medications. Ellen said, "God, I must look terrible. I haven't had a haircut in at least six months, and it looks more and more gray each day."

"Considering the circumstances, I think you look remarkable," I offered.

A funny little smirk appeared on Ellen's face, that I am sure she had in abundance at one time, when life was not so complicated and precious. A year and a half of this nurse/mother keeping her beloved son alive, against all odds. We had talked many times of the dilemma of modern medicine. The ability to keep some one alive, kind of, but the inability to solve the mystery of this rare and deadly disease. Keeping him alive if only a chance of a medical breakthrough … or a miracle.

Ellen had dutifully prayed for a miracle for Vince, as had her church, as had countless friends, relatives, and caregivers. Vince marched steadily toward weakness, and now unresponsiveness. His breathing had reached such a state that that it only occurred about once or twice a minute. Vince, as a living human being, was only measured in the ability to somehow breathe at all. The ventilator left, thank God, a few months back. Ellen had accepted it in her head, but not in her heart. Her training as a nurse told her death, and the ventilator, was only a promise of "not Vince."

God was not responding to the miracle request. Her precious child was dying. Was this lack of God's miracle a response to a betrayal, a sin of the past, an uncaring God? We went down many of those trails together over the last four months. The simple truth, we will never know the answer to those questions until another time.

Ellen's family took shifts with Vince. For eighteen months, every sniffle, sigh, heartbeat variation was discussed, analyzed, and dealt with by Ellen, and her family. For what reason? Because of love. Love of a son, nephew, friend, cousin. Love of hope. Love of possibility. Love of having one more minute.

We drank our coffee, talked of God, and a monitor beeped. Ellen leaped to attention, rapidly moved in to the living room/hospital room. The caregiver, Kim, said, "It is the clogging again in the trach." As if a violin section in a Hayden concerto, the movements of the players were quick, flowing, and precise. The clog resolved with some suction, allowed another minute of breathing.

I walked in and watched.

Ellen quietly stroked Vince's shock of overgrown black hair. A hair that looked way out of place on this ever-thin body, alive only to keep the disease alive. She crept up in bed and curled up next to him, holding him, telling him he was loved, kissing him gently, and she closed her eyes.

I said, "Call me if you need me, my prayers our yours. God bless, Vince." We had prayed many times for miracles, for strength, for understanding for peace.

Peace was found by Vince early the next morning, while being held by his mother Ellen.

I placed this story in the section of Agency, because it was exactly what Ellen needed to do for her son. Eighteen months of intensive care, in her home, when all in the medical field urged her to just allow him to die. Did she add a year, a month, a day, an hour, or a minute? I do not know.

This was a mix of Ellen's needs, as well as Vince's needs. But I know for sure that Ellen did exactly what she felt she was called to do, and that is what she did with her life.

We are never in a position to judge another's motivation or Agency. We just do not know what we would do in the same situation. Would we listen to others, or do what we felt was right and true in our own hearts. As I watch people cope with these awful choices, awfully difficult decisions, every decision is Agency, even if it is a decision not to care. In each decision, we build a list of actions that are one day to be reviewed, if we are lucky in hindsight, with a lot more clarity.

I might not have agreed with all of Ellen's Agency, but I sure as hell admired it.

Agency

The Second Career

We make a living by what we get, we make a life by what we give.

– Winston Churchill

"I like the young line that they have. They may have two freshmen there, but they will grow into their jobs. Give them a year in the SEC, and watch out." Hope springs eternal in a college football fan. And RJ was a football fan. And RJ knew his team. A season ticket holder to "Ole Miss," he rarely missed a game, and he lived for the football season. All summer he studied the recruits, the transfers, and the returning players.

"They never could get their running game going last year, because of those two positions. These guys will help, and that will keep the blitzing down." RJ went on to muse and analyze as we shared the cup of coffee he had made me.

"Well, I guess I should see if Liz is ready for lunch." Lizzy was his mother-in-law.

RJ was not a small man, he smoked incessantly (about the only thing I did not like about my visits), and his middle-aged stomach was showing some growth.

As he moved up to Lizzy's hospital bed, strategically located in the dining room of RJ and Sue's lovely home in northern Mississippi, he called out, "Lizzy, you beautiful lady, are you ready for some lunch?" He gently lifted her out of the bed, carefully as if handling a crown jewel, and tucked her into the wheel chair. He took a washcloth on the overnight stand next to her bed and wiped the accumulation of crust that had accumulated on her eyes. With that he wheeled her into the dining room where I was sitting.

"Hi, Ms. Elizabeth. What is your life like today?" I offered as she looked blankly out at me, trapped in her fourteenth year of Alzheimer's. No sound, a few blinks of the eyes, no more.

The bill of fare was some mashed potatoes, some Jell-O, and some carefully ground-up beef for protein, then chocolate pudding. I prayed the blessing, the microwave beeped, the sumptuous fare was delivered, and RJ began the feeding. Lizzy slowly took the food offering, sometimes easily, usually with prodding. RJ was an expert; it had been seven years since he retired from his auto parts store, which he had sold. He had made a good deal on the sale, and was able to retire around the age of fifty-one. He envisioned a retirement of fishing and golf, visiting old buddies, and friends on trips, and of course a bunch of Ole Miss football. Then Lizzy in her assisted-living facility changed, she stopped eating, and became hugely disoriented. RJ and Sue had to decide on some plan.

RJ said he would try to care for Lizzy on a trial basis. That was seven years ago.

RJ has a lot of energy, and, he willingly admits, some days he gets buggy. But he said that he discovered in himself something he never thought existed when he worked in the helter-skelter world of auto parts. He could deeply care.

RJ was never much of a religious man, had no burning desire to carry a torch of purity for anyone, but due to some strange cosmic twist, he was given the opportunity to care for an Alzheimer's victim. This ninety-three-year-old wisp of a woman he said was never a special mother-in-law. "She was okay, and I got along with her. But she needed Sue and I, and I was available, so ..." RJ explained one visit.

Lizzy finished her wonderful lunch and even smacked her lips on the chocolate pudding. Her royal wheelchair took her into the family room, her favorite chair, and endless stream of soap operas quietly changing scenes on the quiet tube. RJ hated to admit it, but he said he had become hooked on *The Young and the Restless*.

"What are you going to do, when Lizzy finally goes?" I inquired, as I am always concerned for the loss of identity for long-term caregivers. It is sometimes much more difficult for them, as it is two losses.

"I don't know, maybe go back to work at another auto parts store. They have asked me. We will see. Sue will retire later this year. We have some decisions to make. We'll see." RJ glanced off, and a tear found his cheek.

"You okay, my friend?" I softly said.

"I don't know," he said as a sniffle escaped. "I don't really want to think about that time, although I am tired." Lizzy coughed. We turned to look; she dozed off to sleep.

"I bet you are. RJ, I never have seen the type of care you give Lizzy. You are a remarkable gift to her. You know that."

"I know," he said after a sigh, "and she to me."

The following week, Lizzy took another turn and passed in peace with RJ and Sue at her side.

We are defined in our society, especially us men, by our job. That is wrong. I think that we are largely defined by unwanted situations. It is in the unexpected times that we get defined. It is like all the older men that have served in WWII. That situation, unwanted, defined a generation.

RJ was defined by an unexpected and probably unwanted occurrence. This southern man, all man, who loved "Ole Miss" football, a good drink, a good time, was subtly shaped by a woman who weighed less than eighty pounds. RJ and his Agency was indeed in his capacity to act, " … a generative force that inevitably leads to the matter of call." RJ was called, unexpectedly, undesired. It created a life given, in his act of Agency. Now let us turn to another cause that can speak to all the stories thus far, that of blessing.

BLESSING

BLESSING: Affirmation of another at a deep, primal level of being; blessing can be given or received from another, but one cannot bless oneself; integral to blessing are connection, coherence, and agency; thus blessing leads to action and hope seeking healing change with others.

Some years back, I sat with my one-year-old grandson in my lap. It was the season of Thanksgiving, and I indeed felt blessed with my family around me, a nice home, a good job, and, as my mom always said, if you have your health you have it all. The concept of connection, coherence, and agency were all employed. I felt blessed.

The phone rang, and it was from the parish where I served. The parish staff wanted to let me know that little Madolyn had passed away at the age of seven months old. They thought I would want to know since I had baptized her not more than a month ago. Madolyn had suffered from a rare skin disease that allowed her to be bruised with the slightest of touch. The baptism was a blessing to me as well as the family. Now this little one had died. I looked at my grandson Jensen in my lap, and as sad as I was for that family, I felt an overwhelming sense of blessing. I was blessed to be able to hold my sleeping grandson, feel his warmth and trust. And part of that blessing and all blessing is the full knowing that blessing is in knowing that the permanence of life is very transitory. That was probably the biggest blessing I received that day.

We can only have a specific blessing, and then it is gone. You cannot bottle or can it, you may be able to feel the sense of blessing or experience blessing again, but never in the exact same way.

Our first story of blessing was a rare moment of blessing that changed things for me.

Blessing

Glory to God

Dying is a part of life, not in opposition to life.

Fr. Richard Rohr,
Sermon on the Mount Audio Tape

I received the call to get to the hospital that day if I could. Ms. Rice was dying, and the family wanted some support.

As I entered the hospital room, a vibrant woman was sitting up in bed, looking straight out at me. This was not a typical hospital visit for a hospice chaplain. Usually, it is a barely breathing person, seeking breath with full purpose, the only action left to a person.

"Hi, Ms. Rice. I am Chaplain Jack Conrad. You look like you are doing very well."

"Glad to meet you, Chaplain. Great to have you here," she spurted with great enthusiasm. Her daughter, Sandra, was right there at her side; a friend, Simone, was also there from her church. "Isn't it great to have all these family and friends here …" and Ms. Rice went on for at least fifteen minutes. I wondered how such a spirit in a woman could be encased in such a pale, disease-ridden body that was obviously in the last stages of decline. Her IV was hooked up, her legs were swelling, but it was the relentless beast of cancer in her lungs that was slowly choking life from this lovely, wonderful person. "Don't you agree, Chaplain, that God has in his own way gifted us all that way?"

"Ms. Rice, I could not agree with you more," I responded, noting her eyes that were dramatically bright and alive now drooped, as it seemed all her body did simultaneously. I asked, "You look tired. Perhaps we could share prayer, before you take a nap?"

"That is a great idea!" Ms. Rice seemed to wake again.

Now in all of my visits, probably 99.9% of the time when I suggest that we pray, I am the one that leads prayer. Not this time. By the time I took a breath, attempting to settle myself in the Lord, Ms. Rice launched into prayer.

"Glorious God, I give you thanks and praise for all my family, for ..." It rolled from her lips as it rolled from her heart. "And Jesus, we all know that you are the promise, and we give our prayer in your name, that precious name of Jesus, for the Glory of God. Amen. Now I'll take my nap." And just like that, she fell asleep. I stood there stunned.

Her daughter Sandra looked at me and smiled. "She has been doing this for two days, Chaplain. She awakes, holds court, then goes off to sleep." Ms. Rice was a female dynamo that gulped big of life, had been a member of her church for eighty-five years. That's right, eighty-five years. She was five when she started. It was now a mega church, and every major pastor, assistant pastor, associate pastor, and clerk had come to pay homage. This woman knew connection, knew coherence in her faith, and God knows had enough Agency to light New York City on New Year's Eve.

I spoke with Sandra and Ms. Rice's friend and got a bit more of an idea of the seriousness of the health crisis; Ms. Rice had maybe a day, no more. I promised to get back the next day when the other of Ms. Rice's children were due to come in.

Precisely at 12:30 p.m., I arrived. Sandra and her sister Emily were holding Ms. Rice's hand, and tears flowed from both of them.

I said "hi" quickly, hugged Sandra and then Emily, who were just introduced.

"Jim is on his way. He should be here any minute now," Emily offered about their brother.

I turned to Ms. Rice; her breathing was very shallow, and her face ashen, and her fingernails were turning blue. I offered to pray, which was richly welcomed, and as I came around the side of the bed, the door opened and Jim walked in, came directly to his mother. I started to bow my head when Ms. Rice opened her eyes, looked out to somewhere where we were not allowed to see, and spoke.

"Glory to God, glory to God, glory to God!" Then she closed her eyes and died, collapsing back upon her pillow, with a peace on her face that I have seen far too seldom in my life.

At that moment I stopped believing there was a heaven, and from that moment on *knew* there was a heaven.

We all silently stood, in shock, in wonder, in a moment of blessing that would stay with us all of our lives.

Blessing moments sneak up and surprise us. They cannot be planned or liturgized. Oh, we will call them blessings, but those are the generic types. The real thing is a surprise. It is like in spring after a long winter. The bleak days drain life and hope from you, and suddenly, on a bright day, you see the first daffodil, or lily. A blessing cannot be planned; blessings are just meant to be experienced.

Ms. Rice's blessing came to all of us in that room, for we got a glimpse into the promise. A slight snapshot of what God has in store for us all. Those moments that allow the veil to part, and a look from God is granted. Gunderson and Pray say it is "at a deep, primal level of being." And that moment does change you, forces you on with a new-felt energy, new-felt hope, for life and with a purpose.

These moments of grace find us, usually unaware and from the strangest of places. The next story speaks volumes to that.

Blessing

The Richest Blessing

As men, we are all equal in the presence of death.

Publius Syrus (ca. 100 BC),
Moral Sayings

There was something wrong, Greg could sense it. This pain was not going away no matter how many bottles of wine were consumed; it was always there. His only respite was an alcohol-induced sleep that lasted far too short. He found the hospital from one of his newest best friends, Bill, and went to emergency.

He was given a bed, and a diagnosis. Liver cancer. He would be dead in months. Simple, straightforward, no great fanfare. Did he have any relatives? Yeah, a brother in St. Louis. But Greg had not had any contact with him for—what was it, oh, at least four years. The hospital had turned Greg over to hospice, and Greg was living with that newest best friend Bill in a trailer park located inches from despair.

He shook his head to me, in the dingy trailer that was way too hot for anyone, much less for someone who was dying of cancer. He had struggled along for many years on the road until he came to Memphis for some reason even he could not remember.

The social worker Peggy was there with me, and patiently listened as Greg told his story. She had asked me to go with her on this visit, as it was in a neighborhood, if that was in some way a name for it, that was not all that "well thought of." She took her notes, I gazed into his face.

One after another, Greg smoked his cigarettes, lit one from the other, a continuous process. He rolled his own, a personal preference developed over the years. Bugle tobacco. As toxic as the alcohol, now claiming its reward in Greg's pending death. Odd thing about addictions, they kill that what they need for life. Addiction has no life, save the victim. Death solves all addictions.

We learned his basic story; Peggy received a call, and quietly excused herself. I sensed that this loving woman, who had an immense capacity to care, was thrilled to leave. Perhaps it was the cockroaches or mouse droppings. Either was ample reason to not want to be here in a hot little disorganized trailer that was occupied by three men, all of the same type of story. Bonded together in this sweltering box on wheels, stuck in life where no one else could possibly wish to be.

But Greg was glad to be here; it was at least a place. He had been without a place for quite a while, when "on the road." Searching for a place. Forty-eight years of searching for a place.

When Peggy had made her exit, Greg and I sat. He streaming his cigarettes, me listening and sweating. My collar was soaked, and I would have given most anything to loosen the tie that strung around my neck. "So what does a chaplain do, anyways?" Greg ventured, and offered a smile without a full complement of teeth.

"I just come and try to be with you. Are you from any faith?" I asked.

"I am Catholic, raised Catholic at least. Mom used to drag us off to church. I was even an altar boy for a while. But it has been a while, Chaplain." Greg chuckled.

"Do you still believe in God, Greg?" I asked.

Greg gazed at me with an honest grin. "When you are walking along a lonely road with two cents in your pocket, all you have is God."

I sat in awe of that wisdom and faith. It is easy to judge someone who seemingly has taken his life a path not much respected in the world's estimation.

Over the next several months, as Greg's disease progressed, the liver quietly giving way to the ever-demanding cancer that had taken up residence, Greg could barely just lay on the bed. We convinced him that he needed more care than Bill could give him; in honesty Bill wanted him out. He paid no rent, and made no money for the elixir. Greg reluctantly agreed. We found a nursing home for him.

The two words "nursing" and "home" are grave misnomers for this place where people, poor people, went to die. A warehouse for the "not exactly dead yet." But I was diligent in my visits, and despite the conditions, I enjoyed seeing Greg. He had a quiet wit, and honesty and humility that I wish we could bottle and give away. He knew who he was. We would talk out in the tiny broken concrete area between the rooms, where he could smoke his cigarettes, of God, his life, my life, and just stuff. As his condition worsened the conversations became more difficult.

Greg had asked me to try to locate his brother in Missouri. He gave me a number, and what he thought was the city. I searched, called, traced, and got onto the Internet, all to no avail. His brother Steve was not there anymore, and would never know that his brother would be dead shortly. Maybe he would care, maybe not. But I wanted to at least do something more for Greg. Some connection, something, anything, before he died. I felt defeated.

I arrived at his new place at the nursing home. And I carried with me the news that despite my efforts no luck on finding his brother. His one wish, short of cigarettes, would not be granted. One more disappointment to add to the tall stack.

I sat on the bed next to him, where he lay. I started with the small talk. Greg was dying quickly. His complexion had changed since the last visit. The desire for a cigarette was even gone now. He slept a lot and lived out the remaining hours waiting for the final relief.

"Greg, I have something to share with you," I started with reluctance. "I have called and searched many, many ways to find Steve, but without luck.

The number was disconnected, and I could find no record of him in any of the cities we talked about. I am really sorry, Greg," I grimly informed him. I felt a failure.

And then a remarkable thing occurred; Greg smiled, and with a huge amount of effort, lifted himself off the sweat-soaked bed he lay on. He sat upright next to me, looked straight at me, sensing my disappointment and failure, and as if having felt that feeling so many times in his life, he put his arm around my shoulder and said, "That's all right, Jack. I know you did the best you could." I saw in his eyes the compassion of the man I was supposed to represent, that Jesus fellow. I was the one who was supposed to bring the good news to him, I was the one who was the clergyman. Greg did the blessing.

Here the man at death's door, the man who had given his life to dissipation, this prodigal son had become the loving father to me. I was immensely touched and humbled. He had given me one of the richest blessings of my life.

Greg died the following week when I was away. I never got to see him again. The poorest of the poor are buried unceremoniously in a joint gravesite. I miss him.

It is easy to believe in blessings when our loved ones, when we are worshiped by our offspring or spouse, and they surround us during our last days. That is a great blessing. But blessing is yet so much more. As the definition says, it is "affirmation of another at a deep, primal level of being." That is exactly what I felt from Greg, blessed.

Blessing transcends time and space; it is not spent once, never to be used again. Blessing has an endless quality to it that cannot be quantified and can only be lost if we stop believing that we are blessed.

Bishops and priests have blessed me at ordination; I have had the rich blessing of family and affirmation from so many who have been kind and generous. But Greg's blessing was unique, with a richness so sweet. A dying man's blessing, so close to God.

I think for me, Greg was the response to the twenty-fifth chapter of Matthew's Gospel where the Gospel writer speaks to us of the last judgment. "What so ever we do to the least of my brothers, so you do unto me." Greg was Christ in his most pitiable form, and Christ in the richness of his blessing.

In Hebrew scripture, the other side of the coin of blessing is curse. They are companions. In many of the rich stories, they went hand in hand, from Cain and Abel onward. This next story had some twists on blessing and perhaps a dash of curse.

Blessing

Of the Secrets of Pixies

Life is an unbroken succession of false situations.

Thornton Wilder

"There they are, right there," Julie said to me as she showed me the pictures from the album. "That is the Pixies' home. How they got there, we have never been sure, but there they are, for the record. Like I told you, they are out there in the back area, about a hundred yards into the trees. We have pictures of them too."

Julie had spoke of the Pixies before. The trouble was, the stories were not told with a knowing nod of the head or a wink of the eye. Julie and her husband Bob were good at this guise.

"See!" she exclaimed. She showed me another picture of the little hollowed-out log that had the "wee" furniture in it, and right to the left of what appeared to be the entrance was a bright spec of light, or a glow, or something. I did not want to stare too hard, lest this lovely woman might mistake my stare for disbelief. Julie had a brain tumor, after all, and if this is what made her last days better, so be it. But what was being offered as proof looked very suspicious to me.

Bob entered the room, "Ah, looking at the Pixie pictures, are you? They are something, aren't they, Chaplain. It took us a long time to start believing them, but they sure are there." Now Bob, although much better off than Julie, as far as health was concerned, still showed definite signs of dementia, as I had spoke with him off and on.

"Got the Pixie pics, grandmother?" chorused Angela, the thirteen-year-old granddaughter. I was convinced this was a joint grabbing of the chaplain's leg.

Angela sat down, devoured the pictures, the stories flew, the legend grew. I thought I had stepped into a different dimension.

"Want to go out and see their home?" Angela queried me, with the straightest face I had every seen.

"Maybe later, Angela. I wanted to talk to your grandmother a bit longer if I could," I responded.

"Their house is really cool. Okay, see you later," she said as she went out the room.

I never really have a mission on visits, but I had wanted to speak to Julie, and talk of her brain tumor that was advancing. From the first visit on, I felt like I was in a dual dimension with Julie. It took several weeks for our first visit to occur at all, as she would put me off, but the visit was pleasant. During the second visit, Julie broke down and sobbed in my arms about her pending death. The next visit it was if death was as far from reality as could be anticipated, as we went to stories of going on a trip to far-away places. But the time was growing short. The tumor was so large now, that it caused the expensive hair wig on her head to be very disfigured.

I had several phone calls from the various children, who were in a bitter legal fight over who was going to control the family money after Mom died. It was not harmonious, and everyone spoke in private, but no one together. The tensions were growing high, and Bob was suffering each day. It never got spoken, but there seemed to be infidelity somewhere in the past with Bob and Julie. But there was hurt, deep lasting hurt. Some bitterness lingered in each person of this family.

A common aphorism in hospice is, "They were screwed up before we came, and they probably will stay that way, long after we are gone." There was enough work in this family to keep a team of therapists and psychiatrists busy.

My supposed mission this day was to try to help Julie, for I could see the pressure of her denial building. I hoped to be the one to help, if I could. I was sensing her desire to talk when the housekeeper came in on us and brought up the Pixies.

"I think I better lie down," Julie said, and with that she disappeared into her bedroom. Bob sat on the couch.

"What do you think, Chaplain?" he asked.

"It is getting close now, Bob, you know that, don't you? I am sorry, Bob."

With that Bob teared up, sat and looked downward, looked up at me, and said, "So what do you think of the Pixies?"

I prayed with Julie and Bob on Julie's last day. I was at the funeral; spoke with each of the kids, individually of course. I came by to see Bob after the funeral. But there was so much that went unsaid in that family, so many secrets, so much pain, much less the "Pixies."

In the Catholic tradition there is a song that has this phrase, "Our blessing cup is the communion of the blood of Christ." The cup of salvation, the most wonderful blessing known to Christianity, is a cup of blood, and it can be called a blessing cup.

Sorrow, hurt, pain, and lies occupy far too many homes in this world. In search of blessings, we find substitutes, falsehoods, and just plain sin. I did not feel blessed by Julie and Bob's family, and that is sad. Too much deceit, and too much pain in their lives, too much unsaid. I never want to meddle in people's affairs, I just want to be present, and perhaps bring blessing to those in need as they face the reality of death. Months after Julie's death, extended family would talk to me about them, all with questions. But no answers, no blessing. Over the six-plus months of association, no blessing, just questions … like, were the Pixies real?

Now one last story of blessing than was not explainable.

Blessing

Pennies from Heaven

*Never knock on Death's door: ring the bell
and run away! Death really hates that."*

Matt Frewer, as Doctor Mike
Stratford
in "Doctor, Doctor.

"Dad always said, 'Penny for your thoughts,'" Samantha had told me on the phone when I had called her after I heard that her father Matt had finally passed. Darlene, the hospice nurse, had been there earlier, and had been with Matt when he died. I hurried to the home to offer support prior to the removal of Matt's body.

"Throughout our lives together," Sam added, "he would always give me bright new pennies, she told me, for luck and blessing. So somehow, I thought that it would be a great thing to make sure that he had pennies in the penny loafers that we wanted to put on Dad. We could not find them. We looked and looked all through his closet, in the attic, and we could not find them."

Finally, Jerry (Samantha's husband) yelled out to me, "Guess what I found?"

"Where did you find them?" I asked. Jerry said he found them out on the porch in Dad's favorite rocking chair, and they were freshly polished, and inside the front part of each loafer were two bright new 2007 pennies. We through out every possibility. Could it have been their mom or Ron or anyone else? "But this was my thought: no one else even knew about pennies, much less Mom, who was not well, and Dad had been unconscious for a week. Those shoes were not on that porch chair yesterday."

"Wow!" was about the best I could get out. I spoke with each family member; they all told me thanks for all the time, and how much Matt had enjoyed and respected me. They said they were all right and wanted me to be at the funeral, which I said I would really attempt to be at.

I decided to call Darlene the nurse, because I knew that she too was close to Matt and the family, but the phone rang in my hand; it was Darlene.

"Hi, Darlene. Are you doing okay?" I asked. Then we discussed the penny loafer mystery. She said she was there when they finally found them. Too strange.

I hung up the phone, after seeing that Darlene was doing all right with Matt's loss, when the phone went off again.

"You are not going to believe this. It is the weirdest thing." Darlene spoke in a rapid, almost hyperventilating voice. "I just stopped to get gas, and I looked down as I got out of the car, and there right where I stood, was a bright new penny, 2007, not a smudge on it. I think Matt has some pretty strong connections here somewhere." She laughed a nervous laugh. We talked a bit and once again hung up the phone.

As I shifted to get out of my chair, I felt a pinch in my left thigh. I thought, *It can't be my keys or change*, because I always empty my front pockets out into my desk when I come in to the office. I reached in my pocket, and there was a bright penny, glistening copper in my hand. I looked down and checked the date. Of course it was brand-new 2007 penny. I laughed, and began to dial Darlene's number.

I do not tend to be superstitious or supernaturally oriented. I know that God can do all things. But as we shared our penny stories with family and friends at the funeral, we were not the only ones that had penny stories; it happened at least ten different places to different people. A calling card from beyond life as we know it, or a blessing from Matt letting us know that we really do not know very much at all.

A close friend of Blessing is Hope; let us now explore the crucial nature of Hope as a cause of life...

HOPE

Hope: More than wishful thinking, hope is leaning into the future with anticipation fully aware of reality; a process rather than an event where one thrives in the midst of whatever challenges and adversity is at hand; "riskable expectation."

To speak of hope and death seems so contradictory. Yet in my experience Hope springs up so often, I usually expect it with people, especially those that live on past a death. We have to be able to visualize a world without the person who dies. How we envision that time is crucial to define often our lives going forward. But also, like the situation with Stu in the first story, it is part of the one that is dying. I have told many that no one dies without a theology. We all, no matter what our upbringing, have some concept of God, and have some concept of an afterlife.

My first story is of one of my all-time favorite people in my life. Her name was Mary. She was a patient, but this part of her story is about "leaning into the future."

Hope

What you have to do, you do

*Be open to your dreams, people. Embrace
that distant shore. Because our mortal
journey is over all too soon.*

David Assael, *Northern Exposure*,
"First Snow," 1993.

We always sat at her kitchen table. This is where Ms.
Mary sat. Occasionally, her husband Bob would be
wheeled in to sit in the family room that was next
to the kitchen. Bob had Alzheimer's for the last
five years. Bob ate, Bob sat, Bob moaned. But after
fifty-six years of marriage, Bob was always as close
as possible.

Ms. Mary was a devout Catholic, a matriarch, a
wife, and a beacon of hope and possibility to all who
knew her. Mary was dying of CHF, COPD, and a
host of other maladies that were robbing her of precious days. She had four kids, lost one tragically in
an accident. Her one daughter had gone through a
bitter divorce, fought addiction, and somehow was
coping, somewhat. Her oldest son followed as a fire-
fighter as his dad. He was solid and dependable, very
devoted to his mom and dad.

The topic today was Keith. I knew all about Keith
from church. She worried most about him when she

was gone. Mary knew it would not be long for her. With all that still remained going on in the family, what would happen to Keith? Long-term caring of him would be necessary, but how? Rarely was this lady down, but this moment was one of the times.

"We knew Keith was going to be a challenge," Mary started, "between his hair lip, and his limited sight, not to mention his hearing, his diminished mental functioning, and his inability to speak, we knew. Looking back, Keith took the better part of our lives for over twelve years. When we had him analyzed at around five, the 'experts' told us that Keith would not ever speak, hear, and would have to be institutionalized for the rest of his life. We would get to visit." At that Mary chuckled. Mary had the type of chuckle that warms the heart, lifts the spirit, and creates the knowledge in those that hear it that knowing is right behind the chuckle. Mary knew herself, her family, and her God. Her chuckle usually was a laugh at life.

With that chuckle, she paused, and got deeply serious, in the remembrance. "No one was going to tell me that my son would be denied life, because of some tests. I knew my son, what he needed was a school that could work with him, like I was doing at home. Keith was bright, I knew it."

Mary leaned into the future. Had Hope beyond the obvious. As one of the founders of Madonna Day Care, which has now become Madonna Learning Center in Memphis, Mary worked as a volunteer, organizer, teacher, and patron, to help live out what is now listed as the mission statement of Madonna Learning Center:

"Madonna Learning Center provides a Christian environment where children of all faiths with special needs are educated to reach their full potential."

Keith started speaking at the age of ten, went on and finished high school, and some college, and has held a job with the Navy Human Resources Department for close to twenty-five years.

I know Keith as a lector in the church. He is an inspiration.

Mary spoke that day with a conviction that not only dealt with the adversity of life with Keith, but with all the adversities, the loss of a son in a terrible accident, a daughter in crisis, and a husband with Alzheimer's. Mary looked at me that day, after telling me the full story of Keith.

I told Mary, "You are one remarkable Lady, Mary."

Again the chuckle escaped. "No, I just know that God cares, and if you believe, there always is a way."

Mary grew worse, she lapsed into bed, and during the visits still she would chuckle and delight me. She embraced a different hope now, the hope of her family without her. One of the last days that she was still lucid, she looked at me, and the look that she had that day a month or so back when we last talked about Keith returned.

"What will happen to him?" She looked at me.

"Gotta keep up the hope, Mary, you told me that," I said. The chuckle again.

"I will keep an eye on him, Mary, I promise. You know you have done all you could, have some faith in him and your kids, okay?"

Mary smiled, closed her eyes, and said, "Okay."

Keith did the first reading at Mary's funeral. He was magnificent, so was the rest. The church was full to say good bye to this remarkable lady. I had the honor of giving her eulogy.

And I keep an eye on Keith, just as I promised.

Hope is "a process rather than an event where one thrives in the midst of whatever challenges and adversity is at hand; riskable expectation." Mary was that definition. It was that taking a look out to a place that is not, but could be. Adversity after adversity was encountered and dealt with, maybe not perfectly, but dealt with, with faith.

I am not exactly sure why hope resides in some, and not others. But with hope, it makes this life immeasurably more worthwhile. It is incredibly obvious when it is not there. It is like a symphony without the string section, it just is not right.

Hope brings a willingness to go forward. When I see families coping with difficult situations, if they do not lapse into despair, they find hope again, a way outside of what is, a re-imagining of the world in a different state. A drop of hope should never be brushed off, never ignored. That drop could lead to an ocean. Just ask the thousands of kids that were helped at Madonna Learning Center.

Now, what if we hope for something very odd?

Hope

The Rapture

If I could drop dead right now, I would be the happiest man alive.

– Samuel Goldwyn

Rob looked at me, then at Evelyn, his bride of sixty-three years. It was a sunny day, the kind of day in early fall that made you glad to be able to breathe the sweet-smelling air. It was Sunday, and after seeing this great couple over the last month, we had moved to a friendship of sorts, and when I came in, it was a comfortable place to be with these two people.

I was working in a rehabilitation center, and people were there to get stronger, learn to get around their world in a new way, not to die. But Evelyn was sick, and after three weeks in rehab, Evelyn was not only not improving, she was declining. Rob could see it, but refused to admit it. Evelyn knew she was getting worse, and she would not say a word, because she knew it would upset Rob.

Rob was a very bright man, had flown B29 Bombers into Japan during WWII, had done okay in business, and had been healthy and a devoted husband all his life. He was losing her. He would always talk positive, keep up a good face. He had a deep faith, that went back to flying bombers into dense flak, and trusting in his praying of Psalm 91, and especially verses 2 and 4 (NSRV)–"say to the Lord, My refuge and my fortress, my God in whom I trust…under his wings you will find refuge." Four years of praying that and watching his plane remain in the air formed his faith.

Unfortunately, this flight was not one that was going to go well. This was Evelyn's third trip from hospital to rehab, and it was not working.

I left them that morning, and it seemed as if the reality hung in the air. Unspoken, yet taking up all the air. When I left, I felt more needed to come out, when and how I did not know.

I happened to find Rob that morning in the lunchroom, having a cup of coffee, while Evelyn rested. He said to me, "Come and have a cup of coffee with me," and motioned me to a chair.

As I sat down, he looked at me; there was something on his mind. "Don't you think that the end of the world is near, Chaplain?"

Now of all questions that I dislike as a chaplain, this is number one. You are swimming upstream. You do not want to upset someone if they have deep beliefs in this, but in the same way, you do not want to fuel this fire.

"Could be. What do you think?" I parried his thrust.

Rob went on to cite all the happenings in the world that gave sure indication that the end was near. He was on a roll. As he wound down, all I could do was offer the out card in these discussions. "Well, Jesus did say that we never would know the time or the hour."

Rob said, "That's true." But rather than offering another attack, he put his head down, and silently began to cry. "But I want it to happen, I want the end of the world now." As he straightened up, with his eyes red, he looked deep into my eyes.

"Why, Rob?"

"Because I want Evelyn and I to die at the same time. If this happened we could go together. This is what I hope for." He paused, attempted to gather himself, looking into the face of death, of his love that had waited until he returned from all those missions. The mother of his children, the warmth of his bed, the one who shared his life. If only?

All I could say was how sorry I was that this was happening. This brave pilot was not going to be able to dodge this situation. This maneuver of the Rapture would not avoid the obvious reality of having to live after Evelyn died.

Hope is powerful, but it has to also be more than wishful thinking. We can delude ourselves with false hope, embrace it, use it as a shield to fend off reality that we refuse to accept and that we do not want to look at. Hope has to be more than wishes, and it does matter. One day Rob will have to face a new life for him, one without his Evelyn.

But to those that are married for a long time, that have become more than two people, but have become one body, this separation can bring times of no hope. Hope is necessary for life.

We have all heard stories of long married couples dying within a year or months apart. It is referred to as "dying of a broken heart." That will to live, that lack of being able to envision a life in the future without that spouse.

Hope is also something that we have when we do not know why we are hoping at all, and grace finds us. As in this next story.

Hope

Consider the Ravens

Consider the Raven; they do not sow nor reap, they have neither storehouse nor barn, and yet God feeds them. Of how much more value are you than the birds.

Luke 12:24 (NRSV)

Hope can sneak up on us. We may not want to hope, or be seeking it. It can provide itself in very unusual situations. But we do need it.

Amanda was a very nice lady. But living in a nursing home, even a relatively good one, can drain the spirit. The sameness, the smells, the noise, the dying, the sometimes lack of compassion can drain a person's spirit, reduce hope to a silly remembrance of days long gone. Amanda was still fairly lucid, could share life stories, but those telltale nursing-home blues were upon her.

She was sometimes standoffish, sometimes played possum, and just wanted to be left alone. When she was with her sisters, often though I could see the glimpse of what she once was a vibrant, feisty woman.

This day, her sister was there with her daughter. Amanda was talking a bit, and said, "I want to go outside." So we did.

We found a great place, on a wonderful sunny day. But Amanda was restless. Each time her sister and daughter would start a conversation, Amanda was too hot, too cold. She finally said, "Let's go to the courtyard. I just can't get settled today."

Maybe dementia, maybe just crabby. But with the sister and daughter getting frustrated, I took to piloting the wheelchair.

We whisked through the lobby, out the back doors into the courtyard. A pleasant place, except that it was the place of the smokers. I looked around and looked for a place to sit where, hopefully, Amanda would be happy. We took a tour around the courtyard, and I noticed the bird feeder in the back of the courtyard. It was teeming with birds eating, carousing, and just being birds.

On our first approach all the birds scattered; as the humans approached, wisdom sent them to flight. A blink of light came out of Amanda, her head turned and followed the birds.

"Aren't they great?" I offered. "Let's try a different approach."

I slowly made a turn; the birds returned, and I edged up and stopped. Well, close enough to see the birds feed and cavort, but far enough away so that we did not send them to flight. Amanda's face lit up. It was the first real smile I had seen from her in the two months of visits. She sat up, looked with delight. I kneeled next to Amanda and enjoyed the birds' activity with her. The moment of delight was being shared and delighted in. Hope of life crept in, captured us.

"It reminds me of the verse about how Jesus said, 'Consider the ravens.'"

Amanda finished the verse. "'They do not sow and they do not reap ... '"

Then she started to sing, "I'll fly away, old glory, I'll fly away. When I die, hallelujah by and by, I'll fly away." We sang together.

Life returned at that moment to Amanda. The nursing home faded into the distance, and life had meaning, we leaned into it, finding hope that life was worthwhile, and was fun again. These wild birds, from nowhere, helped us find somewhere, kindled the spirit of hope in life that at too many times embraced hopelessness, with the disease in this sweet woman.

A day worth remembering forever.

I can find that my job seems at times to be hopeless. I don't act like it, or show it. I know that my presence to the dying has great meaning, that "riskable expectation." But it can be some long hours next to a non-responsive person who has been in a coma for months or years. It would be quite easy to lose hope, become dejected.

But when the moments find you like the one I had with Amanda, each tough hour is replaced with wonder and joy. I don't hope for moments like these, I don't expect them, I just enjoy and relish them. I lean into the future, and deal with the adversity, knowing that yes, God is at work, and hang on…

Now let's meet Evelyn, the wonder of hope for a wonderful tomorrow that awaits us all.

Hope

The Angel with the Wings Too Long.

There is no such thing as an orderly death. We can sometimes anticipate and have a good inkling as to when someone will finally die, but at best for us hospice workers it always will be just a guess. This certainly was the case for one of the most delightful women that I had ever met, and her name was Evelyn.

It was late on a Monday afternoon that I got the call that Evelyn was becoming "active." Active is hospice lingo for *the patient will die soon*. The breathing changes, the patient responds very little, and physical changes start to occur. Evelyn was dying, and it would be soon.

This had happened once before, but that was six months ago, and she rebounded and came back, and back strong. Well, as strong as any ninety-seven-year-old who hears very poorly and can hardly see anymore. Evelyn was a delightful person. One raised in the South, with the Southern sense of gentility and order. She was raised in a different age, a different time, but time stood a bit still for her. And at this point of her life, why change?

She was also a flirt, occasionally would like a good stiff drink, and had a deep profound love for life, and also for her daughter Darian. And every so often, this precocious part of her personality would peek out from the Southern lady. She would look at me at times, and notice me, and with her very poor eyesight, say to her daughter, "He's good looking!" Once when watching a movie with Cary Grant, she remarked, "Now there is a man I always wanted to be with."

But she was a true, beautiful soul that loved deeply and had a wonderful love of God and her Methodist Church. She would always reverently pray with me, and echo "Amen," and thank me for my "sweet prayers."

Darian was a devoted daughter, and by far one of the best caregivers I had ever seen or experienced. Her devotion for her mother took on a "passion" for her care, and was done not only with wonderful care, but precision and profound love.

When the nurse called me and told me that Ms. Evelyn was getting close, I came. As I walked into her room, I saw her peacefully laying there, her breathing ragged, eyes closed. Darian was tearful, yet prepared. The nurse was checking her vital signs, and indeed her heart rate was changing and blood pressure was falling. I encouraged Darian to quietly talk to her mom, and tell her it was all right and that she was going to be fine. And Darian would lovingly do this, with tears in her eyes, and say over and over, "It's all right, Momma, I'll be just fine. It's going to be all right, Momma."

Then she awoke. Now, it is not unusual for people to make a surge. That is to become awake and lucid, speak out, and then pass on. This is at first what I thought was happening. But Ms. Evelyn was back; her breathing changed, she looked out at Darian, and said, "No, it's not okay! I'm not going to leave you alone. Who will be here for you? I won't leave you alone." These emphatic statements were far from what I would call as normal.

In the next few minutes, in spite our encouragement that it was going to be all right, she would have none of it. "No, no, no, *no*!" she shouted. After about five minutes of this discussion, it quieted down, and Ms. Evelyn started to see something. "Do you see them? They are right there."

She looked out into a place we could not see or go. "Four of them." And she waved a small wave, and her eyes twinkled, as if a young girl looking at a room full of dancing teddy bears. "The angels!" After just a few minutes, her eyes closed, breathing became constant and went to sleep. She woke up five minutes later and ordered a Scotch and water on the rocks, two fingers Scotch, one finger water. It was my first experience of seeing Scotch and water on the rocks in a "sippy" cup.

We all waited for another half and hour, but Ms. Evelyn, as if in a defiant stand against God and Death, had made a decision: she was not going, not now. After prayer, I left, assuring Darian that I would return if she changed.

The following day again she changed, but then rebounded.

On Thursday morning, I went once again to visit. Ms. Evelyn was awake, and waving once more at her angels. The angels were ready, had been sent and were waiting for the final moment. Her waves were so endearing, and would erase the doubt of any atheist as to the reality of Heavenly beings. This went on for quite some time that morning. Then she looked at Darian, and told her that it was going to be okay for her to go with the angels.

She explained that she had spoke with Jesus, and that Darian was going to have a little one with the name of Suzanne, a name which she did not like, and it was okay if she changed the name. Please remember, Evelyn was dying, struggling, yet telling us this wonderful glimpse into her heaven.

Within that last day, she spoke of the Last Supper with one of the apostles needing more wine. She spoke of a reality that was beyond ours. All we could do was enjoy her allowing us a peek into her heaven. But her time had come. She had negotiated with Jesus, Suzanne was coming, Darian would have a companion, and she was at peace.

The last hour, I was not there. Evelyn came to lucidity once more, waved at the angels, and complained that one of the angels had wings that were too long. Exactly why, we will never know. But after that, she settled down and died in Darian's arms.

A week later, I was at another patient's. On her coffee table was a postcard. On the card was the picture of an angel. The most noticeable thing about the angel was that it had very long wings. I asked for the card, took it to Darian, on which I wrote a poem of the "Angel with the Wings Too Long." In the poem, I explained that the reason the wings were long that the angel was carrying the wings for Evelyn.

The following day, Darian called, told me that she was looking for a sign to know that her mother was all right. She told me that when she woke that morning, she read the poem again, and felt washed with peace. She said she knew her mom was in heaven.

Isn't that what we all hope for, life beyond this existence? We can argue theologically about it, and in the final analysis, we will never know until our time comes to go from this life. But we have hope that it exists, with the angels that have too long of wings, and bring them to us.

Hope leads us to belief in the future, in belief in the reality that is bigger than us.

I have a patient that is a poet, a silenced poet as Alzheimer's has claimed her mind. But she has aside her bed poetry books, which I read to her each time I visit. One of her books is from Emily Dickinson, who said it wonderfully about hope in her poem entitled:

"HOPE"

Hope is the thing with feathers,
That perches in the soul,

And sings the time without the words,
And never stops at all.
And sweetest in the gale is heard,
And sore must be the storm,
That could abash the little bird,
That kept so many warm.
I've heard it in the chilliest land,
And on the strangest sea;
Yet, never in extremity,
It asked a crumb in me.

So, we have covered the Causes of Life; now what?

And Then What Happens?

As a well-spent day brings happy sleep, so life well used brings happy death.

— Leonardo da Vinci

In Evelyn's story as well as in Ms. Rice's story, we got a peek into the "after death" experience. Was da Vinci correct? Is it possible to have a happy death, or rather after death? It is the fundamental question that all of us as humans have. There are many books that have been written about near-death experiences. I have met quite a few people. The most universal consensus is that if you do nearly die, and return, you change.

Before I tell my final story, I would like to recount a story recently told by a priest in his homily…

It was the story of two twins, fraternal twins, one a boy, one a girl. As they grew and developed, they started a discussion. What was this life all about? They had a sense that the life that they were leading would end, and that a change would occur.

They liked their lives in the womb, where it was safe, secure, and they had plenty to sustain them. Where were they? Why were they? What was this cord that they were attached to? What did it all mean?

As they sensed the time was nearing due to the tension being felt, and the rumbles that would occur urging them somewhere else, the little boy was filled with fear, and regret that this existence was going to end. How would they live without the cord? Was there going to be a bright light? Would it hurt?

The little girl was excited, she wondered deeply about her new existence. She loved it here but that there was a radically different "out there" was both frightening and exhilarating. She had questions, but a desire, rather than a fear.

As the moment neared, the boy tensed, the girl calmed herself. And then...

Was that not what we might have at least felt? The anticipation of birth into a new life. Now another quick story that I attribute to a tape heard long ago from Father Richard Rohr that I use often at baptisms.

Mommy and Daddy were amused and amazed as their four-year-old Darren asked to speak to his brand-new brother.

"And I want to speak to him alone!" defiantly Darren stated.

As Darren entered the room and closed the door, Mommy and Daddy listened attentively at the door.

Darren crossed over to the crib, stared deeply at his new brother, who was awake and looked out toward his new brother. Darren leaned in and spoke, "Quick, tell me what heaven is like. I am beginning to forget."

We come from somewhere, and we go somewhere. I told the brief sense of blessing I felt when I held my grandson in my lap, when I heard of the loss of the seven-month-old with the rare skin disease. A follow-up to that is that I wound up doing the funeral for that little one. It was not a desire for me to have to do that funeral. What was I to say to anyone with such a tragic loss? After prayer and some help from the Spirit I came up with a simple truth, and a belief that I shared with the family of little Madolyn.

The truth that I spoke was the assurance that in this life, we all get "A Lifetime." That lifetime could be one day or one hundred years, but it is our lifetime.

The belief that I have that attaches to that truth is that "Every Life has a Purpose." Each life has a part in this wonderful web of God's creation. It has coherence in a grander scheme that we can ever understand. It is coherent in the connections that we make, the acts that occur, even if it is only living a few hours, it changes other's lives and influences those our lives touch. We receive blessings, and no matter how much we understand, there is hope that lingers in us. We want to live, love, and be loved, and that alone matters.

My last story gives one more glimpse that allowed me to see what it might be like once I am birthed into another part of my journey of life. Let me introduce you to Jeffrey.

I Wanted to Stay

*A man should not leave this earth with
unfinished business. He should live each
day as if it was a pre-flight check. He
should ask each morning, am I prepared to
lift off?*

Diane Frolov and Andrew
Schneider, *Northern Exposure*,
"It Happened in Juneau," 1992.

It was late in the evening that Saturday. I was on
a twenty-four-hour shift at the hospital, and at
this time of the evening, I wanted to start trying
to sleep a bit, as the average was two to three wake
ups for death calls every night, where a chaplain was
needed.

The beeper went off, and it was the eleventh
floor in the Thompson wing, which was unusual for
rarely is there any one in crisis there. The nurse said
that a patient was requesting a chaplain, and that he
needed to talk.

I knocked on the door, and there found a relatively young, healthy-looking African American
man in his late thirties. I introduced myself; he told
me his name was Jeffrey. From the nurse I learned
that Jeffrey had AIDS and was very advanced.

We traded pleasantries, and then as if shifting a manual transmission, Jeffrey got down to business. "Chaplain, why am I still here?"

I checked my mental chaplain manual, and the answer to that question is not on any page I ever read. So I asked, "Why do you ask that?"

"Chaplain, I have died twice in the last week, and they brought me back. Chaplain, I wanted to stay there. I did not want to come back at all."

"Really. Wow, what was it like?" The chaplain who had entered the room was now replaced by a very willing voyeur, who sat in rapt attention.

"It was magnificent. I never felt that much serenity and peace. It was like being wrapped in warmth that penetrated me to my very soul, my very existence. It was brilliantly lit, and on the hillsides were millions of people singing a wonderful song that just flowed from them. Oh, I wanted to be one of them, Chaplain. I wanted to sing, and be there forever, I just wanted to stay.

"As I came to the gate, my mother and my friend Ed were there to greet me with Jesus. They were so calm and gracious. Ed looked at me, and told me I had to go back. I did not want to hear that, and I spoke to Ed, who just smiled at me and told me that it was not my time and that I had more to be done, before I could come. I felt at peace, but my heart longed to be with them.

"Before I could protest, I suddenly was back with a light burning over me, bringing me back. The second time was exactly like the first. And here I am. But why am I still here? They did not tell me why I had to come back. I want to go back, but I cannot figure out what might be what I have to do or complete."

We talked for almost an hour. He told me of his life, and that there was much he was not that proud of. He had a deep and wonderful knowledge and belief in God, in Jesus, and practiced his faith by working in homeless centers.

"Jeffrey, do you believe that God has forgiven you for all your mistakes in life?" I asked quietly as Jeffrey's life story started to slow.

"I guess if you are a Christian, you have to believe that, and I do," he responded.

A strange look came over his face, almost as if there were a shadow hanging over him. A question came to my mind. "Jeffrey, have you ever forgiven yourself?"

Jeffrey looked at me as his brow furrowed. "Who are you, and where have you been all my life?" Jeffrey's eyes began to swell with tears, as they bubbled over onto his cheeks, and then downward, falling like precise raindrops, so easy, so natural.

"I was meant to be here right now. I don't know if that is what you were meant to do, or complete, but you have been given some time to do . . . to do . . . to do something that only you can do. It may start with your forgiving yourself, letting go of the hurt, and completing what God intends for you."

He looked at me, with eyes that told me of truth that he was seeing for the first time. It was like working a math problem for so long only to have the solution come to you, and you are amazed at the simplicity of the answer.

Jeffrey spoke. "I want to sing, Chaplain. I sing at the homeless shelter, or sang, when I could. I write my own music."

"Can you sing one of your songs for me?" I asked.

I moved to the hills of heaven as I heard this man sing the most beautiful rendition of Psalm 38, the psalm titled "Prayer of an Afflicted Sinner." There are moments in life that I would love to have recorded. That was one of those moments. One of the lines from that Psalm is this: "Like someone who does not hear, who has no answer ready. Lord, I wait for you; O Lord, my God, answer me."

When he finished, I just sat, warm in the glow.

"Jeffrey, you have a rare gift. If you can, use it often, use it for all of us," I spoke.

"Okay, Chaplain."

It was my sole encounter with Jeffrey; he was released the following week. Why he died twice the week before, and why he is well now, I do not know. If his forgiving himself was what he needed to do, I do not know.

I know I got a peek into paradise through him. It allowed me to thankfully be glad that I do what I do. I also know that God, through me, through Jeffrey, connects, helps us to make sense of it, from God's point of view, helps us to know that our acts matter, helps us to see the blessings we encounter, and are, and helps us to hope for heaven, "on earth as it is in heaven."

My Attempt to Conclude

There are worse things in life than death.
Have you ever spent an evening with an
insurance salesman?

– Woody Allen

My apologies to insurance salesmen. But Woody Allen had a point. There are parts of life that are intolerable, and death could be preferred. Ever sat through a timeshare sales pitch? Have you ever had a holiday with relatives you don't really know that well? It is the painful part of life.

However, in my original premise, that Death matters, I hopefully have given examples in the dying process, where how we think, feel, and act, especially about death, and life does make a difference. Does it really matter whether we have two weeks, two months, two years, or eighty years of life ahead of us? We can, to ourselves be life giving, or *cause life*. This does not mean we will extend it. It does mean that the process of living it with connectedness to one another, a coherence where life makes sense, an ability to act in life to bring about what we feel we must be about, be a blessing to others, and them to us, and live in a spirit of hope, can make a difference. Death seems to bring all of this into perspective, to focus how important life is. Death can form lives of those of us that remain.

Hopefully in the stories above, you could experience, like I did, each of the causes of life. Where it was present, there was more to life. When it was absent, life seemed somehow less. It is like a day with or without sunshine. You cannot measure it, but you know there is a difference.

As I have written these stories, I must admit that I have reflected more upon my last days, and what they may be like. I do not dread it, I just look at myself and how I live. There are many times when I do not act as if my life matters, and that is sad. For each second does matter.

I have in past taught classes on spirituality. I often use the example of walking away from a fixed point, then turning and walking toward the point. I liken this to our relationship with God. I use this example to show that either we are acknowledging God or ignoring God, embracing God or detaching from God, it is active. In is never neutral. I do not believe that there is any pause button on our journey. Death is always too near, and the time of our death is closing in upon us as you read, and I type this. We cannot just wait until later to engage life that we have here. It is not an option.

That is what this work has done for me, perhaps just reinforce in me the desire to take each moment very seriously, but not take anything all that seriously.

Living before Dying is exactly what I hope to do. It is in acknowledging a smile as someone passes, petting your dog. It is watching someone in your life that you call special, as they walk or drive away, knowing that they are precious to you. Deciding never to take life for granted. It is a host of things. Most of all to me, it is allowing in myself the ability to stop and value the life given to me.

I mentioned in the start of this book about regrets. I pray that you and I both get a chance to honesty reflect on the regrets we have had in life. However, from this day forward, maybe you and I can create a few less regrets as we live on.

A little lady patient of mine, so near death, blind, barely breathing, reached out her hand to me as I read her a passage of scripture. I took that frail little hand in mine, I was quiet and just sat with her, enjoying the human contact. At that moment, by stopping and valuing life, we both chose living before dying.

References

Dekar, Paul. *Community of the Transfiguration: Journey of a New Monastic Community*. Portland: WIPF and Stock, 2007.

Doerhing, Carrie. *The Practice of Pastoral Care, A Postmodern Approach*. Louisville: Westminster John Knox Press, 2006.

Gunderson, Gary, and Larry Pray. Leading Causes of Life. Memphis: The Center of Excellence in Faith and Health, Methodist LeBonheur Healthcare, 2006.

Mitchell, Kenneth R. and Herbert Anderson. All Our Losses, All Our Grief: Resources for Pastoral Care. Philadelphia: Westminster, 1983.

The New Interpreter's Study Bible, New Revised Standard Version. Nashville: Arbington Press.

Rohr, Richard. Sermon on the Mount. Cincinnati: St. Anthony Messenger Press, 2006.

(c) 1994–2007 QuotationsPage.com and Michael Moncur.

listen|imagine|view|experience

AUDIO BOOK DOWNLOAD INCLUDED WITH THIS BOOK!

In your hands you hold a complete digital entertainment package. Besides purchasing the paper version of this book, this book includes a free download of the audio version of this book. Simply use the code listed below when visiting our website. Once downloaded to your computer, you can listen to the book through your computer's speakers, burn it to an audio CD or save the file to your portable music device (such as Apple's popular iPod) and listen on the go!

How to get your free audio book digital download:

1. Visit www.tatepublishing.com and click on the e|LIVE logo on the home page.
2. Enter the following coupon code:
   4daf-a78b-89e7-9f5c-ef11-a3d1-2cee-c7e4
3. Download the audio book from your e|LIVE digital locker and begin enjoying your new digital entertainment package today!